# METAL DETECTING

An Essential Guide to Detecting Inland,
on Beaches and Under Water

# METAL DETECTING

An Essential Guide to Detecting Inland,
on Beaches and Under Water

*John Clark*

THE CROWOOD PRESS

First published in 2009 by
The Crowood Press Ltd
Ramsbury, Marlborough
Wiltshire SN8 2HR

**www.crowood.com**

**British Library Cataloguing-in-Publication Data**
A catalogue record for this book is available from the British Library.

ISBN 978 1 84797 149 4

**Disclaimer**
The author and the publisher do not accept any responsibility or liability of
any kind, in any manner whatsoever, for any error or omission, or any loss,
damage, injury or adverse outcome, incurred as a result of the use of any of
the information contained in this book, or reliance upon it.

Designed by Magenta Publishing Ltd (www.magentapublishing.com)

Printed and bound in Singapore by Craft Print International

# CONTENTS

Dedication                                                              6
Acknowledgements                                                       7
Preface                                                                8
Introduction                                                          10

1     Developing an Interest in Metal Detecting                       15
2     Principal Types of Detectors                                    23
3     Buying a Detector                                               32
4     Using Your Detector                                             36
5     Identification and Recovery of Targets                          47
6     Safety First                                                    55
7     Clothing and Ancillary Equipment                               67
8     Searching for Sites and Community Opportunities                74
9     Finding Land to Detect on                                       79
10    Metal Detecting and the Law                                     84
11    Inland Detecting                                                88
12    Beach Detecting                                                 96
13    Safety and Equipment for Underwater Detecting                  111
14    Underwater Detecting                                           116
15    Cleaning and Presenting Finds                                  122
16    Outstanding Finds                                              132

Appendices
    One: The Bernard Phillips Report                                 146
    Two: The Society of Thames Mudlarks and Antiquarians             152
    Three: An Introduction to Eyes-only Searching                    158
    Four: Signals Using a Minelab Xterra 30 Detector                 166
Useful Contacts                                                       167
Index                                                                172

# DEDICATION

This book is dedicated to
Dorothy, Susan, Jeremy, Nigel, Ali, Jane,
Imogen, Harvey, Olivia and Sienna

# ACKNOWLEDGMENTS

The author would like to thank the following for their valuable help in the preparation of this book:

The Wyvern Historical and Metal Detecting Society
Pete Hyams for all his help
Ken James for military badge displays and general help
Brian Sherry, Ken Fry and Gavin Fry for each being 'a detectorist'
Louise Crossley for Club work input
Darwin Turner for his field walking report
Dave Philpotts for his Saxon brooch photos
Dave Ebbage for his report on detecting in France
Brian Cavill for photos and Roman finds
Doug Kirk for photos of the gold half guinea
Eileen Coe for photos
Leon Slee for user proof reading and translation
Pat Haigh for illustrations
Sebastion Melmo for Mudlarking report
Thad Loring-Lee for translations
Richard Gosnell for information for ramblers
Bernard and Cynthia Lloyd for proof reading
Bernard Phillips for the archaeological report on the Saxon burial
White's Electronics (UK) Ltd for photos and technical information
Minelab International Ltd for photos and technical information
Swindon Museum for help with images of their displays
Radio 105.5 Swindon for help with presentation
Kyrie Davis for Natural Lifestyle coaching
Jerry Clark for proof reading

# PREFACE

What makes this book different to any other in the field of metal detecting? Well, in my view it is one of the few books to reflect on more than fourteen years of detecting by a husband and wife team. This provides a broad view on many aspects of the hobby and these are reflected throughout the book.

From the moment I was asked to write this book I worried about how to start, having had little experience of writing. Should I open by thanking all those who helped me put it together through their experiences, photos and stories?

Yes, of course I must say a very big *thank you* to them all. I could not have done it without them.

Particular thanks must go to my friend Peter Hyams, who put my name forward to the publishers. Peter provided so much help with the accounts of his Roman hoard and Saxon warrior burial site located on the Downs in North Wiltshire. My thanks also go to all the members of the Wyvern Historical and Detector Society for their help and support, and to the many experts who gave their time and specialist knowledge so willingly.

It was Sue, my wife, however, who came up with the definitive opening line. It had been a dull and overcast spring day in the Murcia region of Spain. She had been detecting along the beaches on the Mediterranean side of a spit of land, while I had been working in the shallow water on the lagoon side. It was the kind of day when without our hobby we would have been stuck in our motor home reading or out spending money to keep ourselves entertained.

When we regrouped later in the afternoon and swapped stories of our finds we found that between us we had recovered: 54 Euros, four gold rings, seven silver rings and a 29 gram platinum ring. In just one day we had found items worth up to one thousand pounds.

Later, while relaxing with a cup of tea on a seafront seat, Sue captured the essence of this book perfectly when she said, 'Oh, what a wonderful hobby!'

*The day's finds: 'Oh what a wonderful hobby!'*

# INTRODUCTION

I have been metal detecting for more than fourteen years and tend to specialize in beach and underwater detecting. During that time I have recovered items of historical interest, various types of artefacts and pieces of modern jewellery that together have contained more than 2.8kg of gold and 7kg of silver, supplemented by platinum and other precious metals. In addition I have discovered the equivalent of well over £21,000 in various European currencies. The introduction of the Euro in 2001 was not to everybody's liking, but it has made my life much easier now I have only one currency to deal with, irrespective of which European country I am detecting in.

Within the book I shall be showing and using metal detectors manufactured by two companies, Minelab and White's. Both make highly competent and respected products that I regularly use.

My friends at the Wyvern Historical and Detector Society share my passion for the hobby. Many of them have found items dating back several thousand years, from small individual artefacts to a hoard of Roman coins. You only have to attend one of our monthly meetings in Wiltshire to see the rich and diverse finds that are on display and also to realize how much pleasure may be derived from metal detecting.

I used to find that, when I took my dog for a walk, people would often pass the time of day with me, commenting about the dog or maybe the weather. Much the same happens when out with my metal detector. Perhaps the metal

*Euro coins from different member countries of the EU. The reverse of the coin indicates the country of origin.*

*Artefacts displayed at a club meeting. (Brian Cavill)*

detector provides people with an excuse to start a conversation? I do know, however, that some of the questions I am most commonly asked when out detecting, whether on farmland, beaches, or in the water, are 'What are you doing?', 'What made you get into detecting?' and 'How can I get started?'

I normally reply that this is the kind of hobby nobody makes you get into. It may awaken a desire and a curiosity that is already within you, but otherwise you may never fully understand what it's about.

Are you the kind of person who promises the children a day at the beach, building sand castles and playing beach games, only to find that by lunchtime it has become a day for beachcombing, fossil hunting or searching rock pools?

If you like fishing, are you especially interested in working out where the fish are and what they will be feeding on? Perhaps you enjoy sea

*I wonder what might be there?*

fishing and study the tides and the currents. In short, do you look forward to the planning that goes into the hunt?

Do you relish the time of year when you can gather mushrooms or blackberries; do you gather windfall apples and fruit? Do you look forward to a glass of home-made sloe gin by the fire at Christmas while remembering the beautiful autumn days when you gathered your natural harvest of fruits?

Do you like to go cockle- and mussel-picking or netting shrimps, planning the trips to suit the tides?

Do you like history and researching subjects or solving problems? Perhaps you are a member of your local historical society?

All of these pastimes require detailed planning and research, local knowledge and the desire to hunt and gather. If you have answered yes to any of these questions, then this book is for you.

There are various ways in which you can make a start, ranging from field walking and searching using just your eyes to buying a detector from the small ads or from eBay. Throughout this book I will endeavour to guide you to an enjoyable future in the hobby and, who knows, it could even be a profitable one. We will meet

other detectorists and the various clubs and organizations devoted to the hobby, and consider the do's and don'ts, both legal and ethical. I will evaluate the different suppliers and the types of detectors they offer. We will look at how to acquire your first machine and where to look, covering options offered by shops, magazine adverts and the Internet – who you can trust and whom you should be wary of.

There is research into the tools and techniques used to recover the items that the detector may indicate are buried in the ground or underwater, the clothing and general equipment we use on land searches and the different items needed for beach and estuary detecting. There is the opportunity to take a detailed look at the more specialized equipment required for underwater detecting.

Help will be found on how to look for land to detect on and obtain the landowner's permission, and how to find other detecting places, even in town centres. There are endless possibilities to help within the local community to further the good name of metal detecting by offering a 'Free Finds Service' to anyone who has lost something of value.

We look at the law concerning detecting and

*These men spend hours picking cockles.*

finds, who administers these laws and what to do if you find something significant. By knowing the rights of ownership and following the correct procedures you can help ensure that both you and the landowner receive the full amounts to which you are entitled. Examples of letters to landowners and tenants are provided, requesting permission to detect on their land, as well as sample contracts for agreements between detectorists and landowners, setting out the terms of ownership of any items that may be discovered. Consideration is also given to recording finds and how to report them officially, if required.

A recent innovation that will be covered is the handheld GPS (global positioning system), which can give a location down to 10 square metres and is becoming increasingly useful.

Throughout the book there is advice about safety and the precautions you should take. I make no apologies in advance if I sometimes repeat this in different contexts where I consider it to be necessary. Although some people may think of metal detecting as a sedentary hobby, certain aspects of it can take us into situations that may be dangerous if we do not understand and follow some basic rules.

I will take you through beach detecting, describing how to understand the tides and read the information the beach is giving, and show you where to search while on the beach. The differing tourist cultures in various countries can have a dramatic effect on the volume and value of your finds. I will help you understand what happens to an item when it is lost and how vast amounts of coinage, gold and silver is to be found on the beaches of shallow inshore waters. This chapter alone could make the whole experience of detecting very lucrative.

There will also be a chance to take a close look at underwater detecting in freshwater leisure lakes, estuaries and in the sea. From

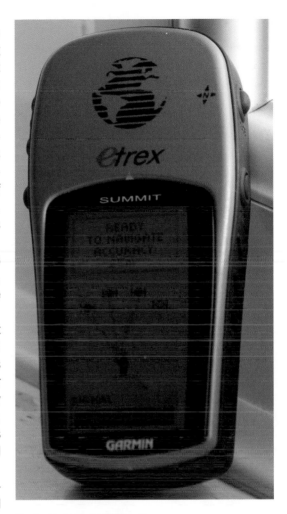

*Typical handheld GPS unit.*

personal experience I can vouch that underwater detecting in the Mediterranean, even in winter, is much more pleasant than the North Sea in summer!

We will look at ways of cleaning and displaying your finds, whether they are delicate artefacts that may be hundreds of years old or modern money and jewellery.

On occasion I have had the opportunity to help improve understanding and general interest in metal detecting within my community by

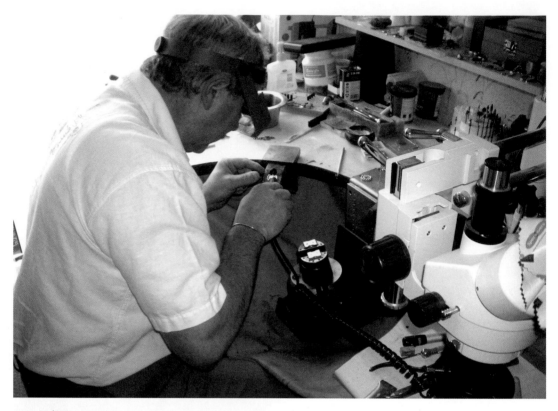

*Some metal detectorists have developed special interests, such as making replicas of ancient artefacts.*

*Shells found whilst beachcombing.*

giving talks and presentations to clubs and other organizations. Recently I have also been asked to put together a monthly radio programme for a local radio station covering all aspects of metal detecting. I hope this book, too, will help spread the word. Welcome to my hobby!

**By definition
'A detectorist is an eternal optimist'**

# CHAPTER 1

# DEVELOPING AN INTEREST IN METAL DETECTING

I have found that most people who get into metal detecting are by nature hunter-gatherers who hadn't previously come across a metal detector. It may take many trips out with the detector before any collectable finds are found. As with many such activities, it is one of the pleasures of the hobby that it can be enjoyed at various levels of involvement.

## MEANS OF SEARCHING

### 'Eyes Only' Searching or Field Walking

In the days before I acquired my metal detectors, I would spend hours searching 'eyes only' on beaches or inland and we still have exotic shells

*Stones have unique and attractive individual markings.*

*Celtic gold stater coin found by a French farmer while walking his fields.*

we found beachcombing on Mediterranean beaches. In addition there are a number of unusual stones brought back from Spain for our garden and some enormous pinecones from the forests of southwest France.

On my detecting trips I regularly see people who are really enjoying their leisure time. Some are gathering a rich harvest of natural treasure, such as fruits, fungi and vegetables, which may be found by gleaning the fields after the harvest season. Others may be taking advantage of the sea's bounty, collecting cockles, mussels and shrimps as well as fishing. Some will be looking for man-made items while field walking, such as pieces of ancient pottery and flint tools, or metal objects such as coins, buckles, musket balls, horseshoes, tools and perhaps even ancient weapons. Many detectorists carry out an 'eyes

only' search of a site before detailed searching with a detector, since often an indication of human activity can be more quickly spotted using this method. Guidance as to the kinds of objects you can find while 'eyes only' detecting is given in Appendix Three.

The Society of Thames Mudlarks and Antiquarians, most commonly known as just the Mudlarks, is a famous and well-respected club in London. It was founded as an 'eyes only' club and has the unique status of being permitted to dig the Thames foreshore at low tide. Although this is a very messy and potentially dangerous branch of the hobby, if not carried out properly, it can be tremendously rewarding and members have made finds dating from modern times right back to the Stone Age. You can read about the Mudlarks in more detail in Appendix Two.

*Mudlark finds from the Thames foreshore.*

### Searching with a Tool

The next logical step after 'eyes only' searching is to use an aid or tool. The first method of detecting using a tool to find what was underground and hidden from sight was dowsing. The origins of the technique are unknown, although it has been claimed that the stone circles at Stonehenge and Avebury in England and at Carnac in France are laid out on so-called 'ley lines', which can easily be detected using dowsing rods.

Dowsing is still used commercially for finding precise locations at which to drill bore holes for water. It is, of course, not electronic metal detecting but it is known that the earth emits a faint electromagnetic field, which, although very weak, can still be 'read' in various ways. There are numerous things underground that can have an effect on the earth's magnetic field, such as water, oil and buried manmade items. Dowsing can identify these changes in magnetism.

### Searching with a Metal Detector

The next step, and the one on which this book is focused, is to go from being a searcher to becoming a *detectorist*! Metal detectorists are patient people who enjoy the chase. In my experience many of them enjoy researching and studying old maps and records; if their intended trip should take them to the coast or an estuary they may also be prepared to check things like tide tables and reports published by the Receiver of Wrecks.

## DETECTING FOR ALL

I recently carried out a survey among members of my detecting club and others with whom I go detecting. While the sample was small, the results are informative about those who take part in the hobby.

- 90% have been 'hunter gathering'
- 50% have been 'field walking'
- 30% are women
- 90% regularly detect on land
- 50% regularly detect on beaches
- 25% have a disability of some degree

Metal detecting is not a strenuous hobby and can be enjoyed by almost anyone from the very young to the more mature. I know of one man in Weston-super-Mare who still beach detects at eighty years old. He says that the detector is a bit like having a dog: it gets him out for some exercise on dull or windy days when he would not otherwise make the effort to go for a walk. At the other end of the age range, on the beach in Torquay I met a young boy of ten struggling

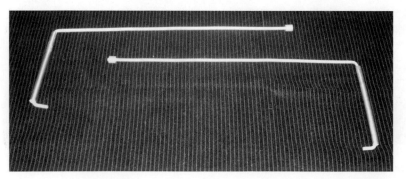

*Modern dowsing rods: dowsing has been used as a search method for thousands of years.*

*I'll show you how to do it.*

with a secondhand detector he had been given. It was not adjusted for his height, he did not have any headphones or digging tools and he had no instruction manual. I provided him with some headphones and a spare beach scoop I had with me, and then spent the afternoon with him and his mother. It was a joy to see his face when he found his first coins. Before it was time to go home he had already talked his mother into getting headphones and other bits and pieces against birthdays and Christmases stretching into the future. He optimistically promised to pay her back with the money he would find on the beach.

For those who are retired and have grandchildren, spending time metal detecting with them is a wonderful way to bridge the generation gap.

I recently had a day out detecting on Southport beach with two of my grandchildren, finding enough money to split it evenly between them. My grandson was very happy as we found some toy cars, and my granddaughter was delighted to have found a 'dinosaur bone'. On returning home she spent an hour trying to find the phone number of the local TV news desk to break the story. It was, of course, a cow's thighbone – but the story will remain a family favourite for years to come. It is a pleasure to be part of a hobby that benefits from having all age groups involved. The older club members certainly find it rewarding to be able to pass on their knowledge and experience to the younger members, though many of them are so quick to learn that they keep us older ones on our toes. In return they help us with various computer programs that are used with the latest generation of detectors. They also assist us in some of the Internet research we get involved with.

Despite its popular image, metal detecting really is an equal opportunity hobby. Almost a third of my club and detecting friends are women and I suspect that many wives and partners detect together. I also know of many couples who go metal detecting and don't belong to the club, so the percentage overall is certainly greater. Modern detectors are much lighter than those produced in the past and do not need a great deal of strength to operate them. Moreover, when it comes to digging to recover finds you only have to visit a gardening centre to see that most of the gardening is done by women. In our distant past it was traditionally the woman in the family group who would do the gathering. I think that in part this is because they often have more patience and tenacity: if I am ready to give up after an unproductive period, it is often one of the women in the group who encourages me to carry on.

*Toy cars are always popular finds with the children.*

*An X-terra 30 Minelab detector in use. They are very light, so will be very suitable for anyone with reduced upper body strength.*

## DETECTING AND DISABILITIES

Many people with a disability can find metal detecting a rewarding hobby. Detectors can be adapted to use a digital meter or flashing light, rather than the normal headphones, for those with hearing difficulties. Blind people can also enjoy detecting, although both they and those who are deaf need an able-bodied companion for safety reasons: a deaf person cannot hear a warning cry or a farm vehicle approaching, while a blind person cannot see an obstruction or pothole. Many years ago I sustained a damaged leg in a car accident. Those like me who have difficulty walking can often manage to amble about on a level beach, or detect in the water where the natural buoyancy helps take the weight off our legs.

For those who unfortunately are more severely disabled and are unable to detect themselves, forming a partnership with an able-bodied person is a possibility. This enables the able-bodied person to do the physical work out in the field, while the disabled partner can clean and

*The buoyancy helps to give support when in the water.*

research the finds. They could also develop the skills to approach farmers and landowners by telephone or letter to obtain permission to detect on their land. Something that almost any of us with a disability can do, with a bit of practice, is to give talks to clubs and groups and help them to appreciate our wonderful hobby.

**Give it a go, you have nothing to lose and everything to find.**

# CHAPTER 2

# PRINCIPAL TYPES OF DETECTORS

There are many types of handheld metal detector available, but all have the following components or features:

- Stem or S rod
- Coil or search head
- Control box
- Display screen
- Battery compartment
- Handgrip
- Armrest or elbow cup
- Socket for headphones

## TERMINOLOGY

Before describing the differences between the various types of metal detectors, it would be useful to run through some of the terminology that you will encounter.

**Ground balance.** A metal detector's ability to ignore the background noise signals caused by metallic minerals. Every metal detector is affected by the mineralization of the ground but the more sophisticated models can deal with it automatically. The balance can change as you move from one piece of ground to the next, both inland and on the dry sand of a beach. Salts and salt water can compound the problems created by ground balance for the detector's circuitry.

**Numerical targets ID display.** A device for displaying a number on an LED screen that always relates to the same signal value. If the operator learns the code number used for each metal type, such as iron, silver or gold, it is possible to identify the metal's composition from the display. In many cases even individual coins of different values can be recognized. It should be borne in mind, however, that there is no common standard as to which number refers to which metal. The numbers assigned vary from one make or model to another. As a result the detectorist needs to memorize the numbers assigned by his or her particular machine.

**Visual targets ID display.** Instead of a number, this kind of display shows a symbol of the item detected. Most of the detectors with this type of meter fitted are manufactured in the USA, but this can cause problems when used in the UK or Europe. Typical symbols displayed when a target signal is received may include a bottle top, a silver or gold ring, and a dollar, nickel (5 cents) and dime (10 cents). Since the composition of such items may not be the same as their British

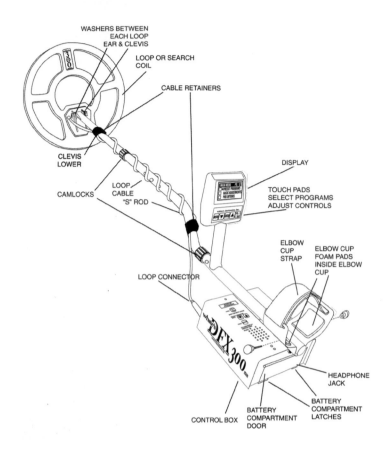

WASHERS BETWEEN
EACH LOOP
EAR & CLEVIS

LOOP OR SEARCH
COIL

CABLE RETAINERS

CLEVIS
LOWER

CAMLOCKS

LOOP
CABLE
"S" ROD

LOOP CONNECTOR

DISPLAY

TOUCH PADS
SELECT PROGRAMS
ADJUST CONTROLS

ELBOW
CUP
STRAP

ELBOW CUP
FOAM PADS
INSIDE ELBOW
CUP

HEADPHONE
JACK

BATTERY
COMPARTMENT
LATCHES

CONTROL BOX

BATTERY
COMPARTMENT
DOOR

*Itemized parts of a Whites metal detector. (Whites Electronics (UK) Ltd)*

and European equivalents (American gold, for example, is normally 22ct, whereas 9, 14, 18 and 22ct gold may be used for jewellery in the UK), these differences can cause confusion in the interpretation of signals, with the result that valuable items may be missed.

**Single tone signal.** The 'beep' heard in the headphones, which indicates that the detector has passed over a target. There is no difference in the tone emitted no matter what the metal it has passed over.

**Variable tone discrimination signal**. A system that delivers a variable tone to the headphones depending on what metal the detector has

passed over. This may, for example, be a low pitch for iron, a mid-range pitch for gold and a high pitch for silver. Many subtle changes in the tone may be generated depending on the metal and the artefact's shape. With diligent attention and practice these differences can be learnt, just as one learns a language.

**Discrimination**. The detector's ability to reject a varying level of 'junk'. This is often controlled by a rotary knob or push-button switch. Too little discrimination and the detector will give a signal for every metal item it passes over, irrespective of what that is. Too much discrimination and it will ignore almost everything. To a certain extent the discrimination control can also be used to

*Numerical display of a Minelab X-Terra 30 detector. (Minelab International Ltd)*

dial out the 'ground interference', but there will be a trade-off in sensitivity.

**Sensitivity.** The detector's ability to 'see' what is in the ground as it passes over it. This is usually controlled by a rotary or push-button switch. Turned down to the minimum the chances are that many target signals will be missed. When turned up to its full extent it will enable the detector to 'see' the maximum targets possible as it is passed over the ground. If it is set to maximum on highly mineralized ground, however, the detector will produce false target signals. With experience and practice the operator will find the best setting for the conditions of the area being searched.

**Junk.** The term given to any scrap metal or unwanted item that may emit a signal, such as old batteries, nails or keys.

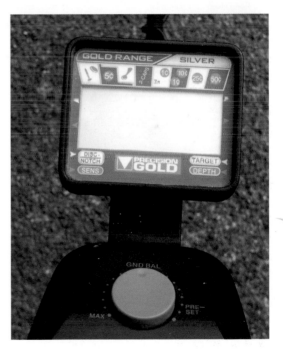

*Visual target display on a low-cost machine made for the US market.*

*Examples of the 'junk' that can turn up.*

## TYPES OF DETECTORS

There has been no shortage of innovative ideas from manufacturers when it comes to applying microelectronics to metal detectors. The three main types of metal detector circuits in use are:

■ transmit/receive detectors (TRs)
■ motion detectors
■ pulse induction detectors

Most people will have come into contact with metal detector machines in their daily life via the walk-through metal detector arches used in airports. The use of detectors in other areas of the security industry has also expanded rapidly, for example controlling entry to nightclubs, football grounds and, sadly, even some schools in inner city areas. Smaller types are even available in DIY stores to enable us to locate wires and pipes safely before putting nails or screws into a wall.

Some specialized types of metal detector are available for non-industrial uses. The so-called Two-Box Transmit Receive/Radio Frequency detector is a machine that can only recognize items larger than 20cm square. Since this type does not pick up small pieces of metal it is particularly useful to treasure hoard hunters and those involved in aircraft archaeology, the term used to describe the recovery of aircraft wrecks from both World Wars. Artefacts the size of an aeroplane engine can be detected as deep as 6m by a Two-Box TR/RF detector but such detectors are of no use in the search for coins, rings and other small items.

Metal detector manufacturers also produce other specialized types that are mainly used by professionals. Among these are magnetometers, which many British readers will have seen demonstrated on Channel Four's 'Time Team' series. They are used to read differences in the earth's magnetism and can detect buried walls, cavities and objects like shipwrecks, which may be deep underground. These machines are expensive, require highly trained specialist operators and are complex to use.

An understanding of the three main types of electronics used in detectors will help you to select the most suitable type of machine to match your budget and the type of detecting you wish to do. The prices suggested were current at the time of writing (2009).

## Transmit/Receive (TR) Detectors

**Price guide:** many available below £100.
The TR is a basic or simple type of detector that transmits and receives a signal even when stationary. Often it has little ability to discriminate between various types of metal. Such machines were first developed in the 1960s. They can be light and have low battery power consumption and therefore low running costs. These are basic machines that can provide a reasonably priced starter detector, but they have the disadvantage that they require constant retuning of their ground balance. They are unable to compensate automatically for changes in ground mineralization.

**Verdict:** TRs can be a great type of detector for children and beginners, suitable purely as an introduction to the hobby. They are fairly cheap and quite easy to learn to use. The TR detector is of limited use on farmland due to its basic electronics and poor discrimination. They are probably best suited for use on dry sand beaches while on holiday. In the hands of an enthusiastic beach detectorist the machine could pay for itself within a few holidays while providing fun for all the family.

*An early 1970s Whites TR detector. These are now collectors' items.*

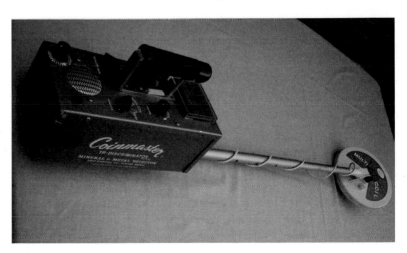

### Pinpoint Handheld TR Detectors.

**Price guide:** £25–£100

These are specialist miniature detectors, comprising a handheld control box with a probe 20cm long, at the end of which is a miniature search head. In technical terms they count as TRs and are favoured by some detectorists as a handy accessory to use when the main detector has indicated a promising signal. The target's exact position can then be pinpointed with the handheld detector. They are especially useful in heavy clay soils and in deep holes, particularly when multiple finds, such as hoards of coins, are encountered.

### Motion Detectors

**Price guide:** £150–£1,000+

Motion detectors have become the mainstay of the hobby since their introduction in the early 1980s. These well-developed and technically advanced detectors have become the first choice within the hobby owing to their superior performance in nearly every detecting situation. They have tremendous sensitivity compared to all other types of detectors and benefit from fully automatic ground balance, which can take care of constantly changing ground mineralization, in itself a major breakthrough. These machines offer a true 'switch on and go' detector for all conditions. As their name implies, however, the coil must be kept in motion and the user must move the detector in an arc from left to right and back again, parallel to the ground, to ensure maximum signal coverage.

All of the better motion detectors have a 'pinpoint mode' to help actually locate the find. This mode is activated by a switch or button and turns the machine into a non-motion (TR) detector.

Many motion detectors incorporate a visual target ID meter or display. These may provide either a numerical or a graphic display. As has been mentioned above, numerical displays are generally better for use in the UK and Europe, since graphic display models made for the US market employ currency symbols for signals that do not equate to the coins we find on this side of the Atlantic.

Some manufacturers provide further user aids. One of the best of these is tone discrimination, a system that turns the single-tone 'beep' used by many machines into a multi-tone sound that varies in pitch depending on the type of metal reflecting the signal. With dedicated practice these sounds can be understood rather like learning a foreign language. It may take some effort, but the rewards can be great.

Between us my wife and I currently have five of these machines. Over the years we have acquired better quality detectors and all of our machines now incorporate tone discrimination; three of them also have numerical target ID. In my opinion these features provide an essential advantage when recovering valuable finds efficiently.

**Verdict:** If you are serious about metal detecting it has to be a motion detector. The 'switch on and go' ability, coupled with the excellent discrimination characteristics and automatic ground balance, make these machines the number one choice for most people.

### Pulse Induction (PI) Detectors

**Price guide:** £200–£900

Pulse induction or PI detectors were the main type used before 1970. They are easy to use and very powerful, receiving signals from a greater depth than any other type of detector.

*Minelab Safari computerized variable tone motion detector. (Minelab International Ltd)*

Their over-sensitivity to iron junk, however, can be a major problem, making them most suitable as specialist beach or underwater detectors. On beaches where there should be very little iron junk, for example where there is hard-packed sand over black sand, on stone beds or maybe on seashell beds, these machines will not receive so many wasted junk signals.

PI machines are particularly useful for going over an area of beach after using a tone discrimination motion detector to recover all the obvious quality signals, such as the money, silver and gold. At the same time recover or mark the plainly recognizable junk signals, such as iron, tinfoil, ring-pulls and bottle tops, using marker flags or sticks. Then go back over the area taking advantage of the power and depth of the PI detector's search mode without the overwhelming burden of shallow junk signals to dig. This will recover targets beyond the reach of the motion detector.

It is worth remembering that it can be quite common for a depth of between 50cm and 1m of sand to be scoured from a beach, estuary or seabed by stormy weather or spring tides in as

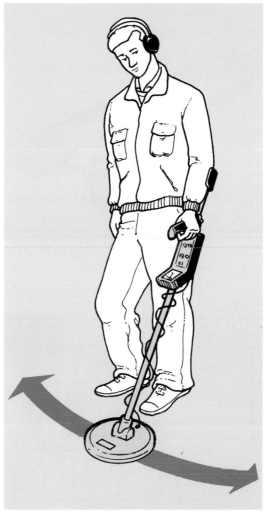

*The side-to-side sweeping motion used when detecting is all important.*

little as twenty-four hours. Under these conditions the use of both motion and PI detectors makes a winning combination.

**Verdict:** The PI detector is the most powerful and deep-seeking machine available to the majority of detectorists. Although they are not necessarily suitable for beginners or for areas with high junk

*The Whites pulse induction dual field detector, an example of a very powerful PI detector suitable for the more experienced detectorist. (Whites Electronics (UK) Ltd)*

*Underwater metal detectors require the user to invest in a large amount of ancillary equipment.*

content, they are a valuable tool for the more experienced exponents of the hobby, when used in the right situation and conditions.

### Underwater Detectors

**Price guide:** £800–£1,200

The electronic circuits used in the underwater metal detectors are the same as those used for the inland and beach detectors, so all of the foregoing information is relevant. The obvious difference between the two types of detectors is that the design of the underwater detector has to accommodate the increased pressure on all the components, which will increase as it is operated further below the surface of the water. The pressure rises by 1 Bar (14.7lb) for every 10m (30ft) the detectorist descends with the machine. One further difference in their construction is they must have the ability to operate reliably in saltwater conditions whilst putting up with knocks, bangs and wave action.

Underwater detectors are undoubtedly expensive, but you must realize that you are in effect taking a hand-held computer into an aggressive and hostile environment and expecting it to operate reliably for many years. Considerable extra research, development and component costs are incurred by the manufacturers, and these are reflected in price of the machines.

### Try Before You Buy

Metal detectors are not necessarily cheap items to purchase. Anyone thinking of buying a machine for the first time should go along to a club or reputable retailer and see if it's possible to try a machine in the field. Some retailers regularly organize weekend rallies and bring along machines for sale. It is then possible to 'try before you buy', with expert advice and tuition on offer to help you make your purchase.

> Don't be in a hurry to buy a machine. Remember that patience is a virtue when it comes to detecting.

# CHAPTER 3

# BUYING A DETECTOR

In this chapter we will look at the types of outlets where you can make your purchase, their advantages and their disadvantages. Before you hurry out to spend your hard-earned money, however, let's look at some fundamental things you need to do first.

## RESEARCH

A good place to start is to buy some of the specialist detecting magazines: the most popular ones on the subject in the United Kingdom are probably *Treasure Hunting* and *The Searcher*. Local retailers who deal in metal detectors will often stock them, together with books on the various specialist aspects of the hobby. Failing that any good newsagent should be able to help.

Reading these magazines regularly should give an insight into the hobby. Within them you will find test reports on particular makes and models of detector, user field-test reports, finds reports, up-to-date information on the law and legislation, adverts, club news and much more. Persuade your family to give you a subscription as a birthday or Christmas present and you will then have the latest news every month. Reading these magazines is by far the best way to build up your knowledge base.

The next logical step is to join your local metal detecting club. Some clubs first invite you to join as an associate member, until there is a vacancy for full membership. One reason for this is that when detecting on club sites the maximum numbers are restricted, for administrative and safety reasons. It does, however, provide an opportunity for a non-detecting associate to accompany a full member and observe the methods and skills employed. This is not necessarily a bad thing, as our first inclination is to run off looking for that crock of gold when actually we should be taking our time and learning the ropes from the more experienced members of the club.

Many members willingly take someone new to the hobby under their wing and help them choose their first machine, both by discussing the options and through field experience. It is not uncommon for individual detectorists to have a 'test ground' where they have buried items so they can practise with their machines and help them learn detailed recognition of artefacts and coins. It would clearly be an advantage if someone were to let you try out several different machines back to back at a facility like this, making it probably the ideal method of choosing the type of machine to purchase.

## WHERE TO BUY

At first glance there seems a mass of ways to buy a detector – magazine adverts, the Internet, dealers, club newssheets and so on. However, for all practical purposes, the various sources for the supply of metal detectors may be divided into trade and private.

The Searcher *and* Treasure Hunting, *the two leading magazines on the subject in the United Kingdom.*

## Trade Outlets

*Manufacturers*

There are not too many manufacturers of metal detectors based in the United Kingdom, so this is a limited category. As they are sometimes run by electronics experts rather than detectorists, they may not always have much detailed field knowledge of their products. Personal recommendation is probably the best way to approach this sector. If there is a manufacturer in your vicinity, however, they might be willing to offer you a factory visit and explain how modern detectors work.

*Importers/sole distributors*

These tend to be small companies importing one make of foreign-made detector. They are often staffed by the proprietor and family or a small staff, and they may sometimes supply other retail outfits. The major advantage in buying from such a company is their in-depth knowledge since they have only one make of detector to deal with and, of course, they will be in direct contact with the manufacturer and fully up to date with the latest models and information. Their main strength, however, is also their weakness in that they can offer only one make of machine.

### Importers/multiple-make dealers

By definition these are the 'big boys' of the trade with hundreds of thousands of pounds worth of stock and a well-trained staff who will almost certainly be active metal detectorists. All of this will take place in large, well-stocked commercial premises. They will also have a resident engineer to carry out tuning and warranty work. Importers/multiple-make dealers can be identified in the detectorist magazines by their regular and expensive advertising. Such companies will commonly offer attractive package deals, accessories and books, all available via mail order and often with the option of interest-free finance.

### Multiple-make dealers

If there is a multiple-make dealer within reach of where you live, a visit to view their range and seek hands-on advice would be a valuable experience. Many firms of this type are well respected and highly experienced, carrying an impressive range of stock that will almost certainly include new metal detectors from the major manufacturers and a selection of previously owned detectors. Many of these dealers arrange and attend rallies where they present their stock and members of staff are available to provide friendly advice.

## Private Sales

Many people first get into the hobby by buying from a private source, perhaps from someone at the club you join, or maybe from the For Sale adverts in one of the detector magazines. Although it may appear to be a cheap way into the hobby, from my experience it is rarely quite the bargain it seems. The biggest problem is that you will not yet have the experience to make an informed decision on which detector to go for.

Second-hand machines are better left until you have some field experience.

People sell detectors for many different reasons. It could be they have invested in a new model, perhaps they have too many detectors and have some duplication, maybe they are giving up the hobby, or perhaps the detector is complex and difficult for them to learn. Whatever the reason, the ground rules when buying second-hand are the same, even if buying from a dealer.

## BUYING A SECOND-HAND DETECTOR

Buying from a recognized dealer will generally offer more protection than buying a detector from a private source. Naturally, the machine may cost more, but you must remember that the dealer has a legal obligation to his customers that would be difficult, if not impossible, to enforce on a private individual.

Whenever possible I would recommend buying from a dealer you can visit in person, because, should you have any problems, it is always easier to sort things out face to face and you will benefit from hands-on advice. If you are considering buying from a rally or show, I would suggest also visiting the dealer's premises to check on the facilities and back-up service.

Once you have made your choice, do not hand over your hard-earned money without some sort of a field test. Make sure the machine is not too heavy. The weight of a detector is very important, since you will often be using the machine for several hours at a time. If your partner is likely to use the machine as well, let them also try it for weight: after recovering from surgery for breast cancer, for example, someone I detect with had to swap to a lightweight detector as she had reduced strength in her right arm.

Always check the serial number. If it is not evident or has been mutilated, do not purchase the machine under any circumstances. If you do, you may even be party to á crime through receiving stolen property. Ask to see any documentation, purchase invoice, receipt, user handbook and perhaps any copies of magazine field tests for the machine on offer. Always enquire after the terms of any warranty or exchange period and whether there is any money-back period if you feel the machine is not suitable for you. Make sure you have the terms and conditions of sale in writing, even from a private individual.

Wherever you buy from, you will be in a stronger position to negotiate for a sensible discount if you do not need to make a part exchange. In case you need it, check out the best finance deal you can make. Many dealers offer interest-free finance but you may be better off using another source of money and securing a 'cash discount'. Many credit cards give an interest-free period on purchases and you need to compare all the offers before you buy.

A few points are worth mentioning concerning private sales. I would be very wary of buying on the Internet or from other sources of adverts unless you can arrange to meet the vendor at his or her home address. Even then do everything you can to make sure it *is* the vendor's own home. Always ask for a landline phone number. Genuine sellers won't mind you carrying out these checks. If there is any objection, or you are only offered a mobile phone number and a meeting at a local pub, walk away from the deal.

> **Remember that if a deal seems too good to be true, it normally is too good to be true.**

# CHAPTER 4

# USING YOUR DETECTOR

By now you may well have acquired a metal detector to suit your needs and your pocket. Naturally enough, you will be itching to get out there and start finding things. There are several aspects of the hobby, however, that are worth studying in some detail before venturing out into the field. For the purpose of this exercise we shall be using a tone discriminating motion detector.

In order to properly understand the information your detector feeds you through the signals it receives, always buy the best-quality set of headphones you can afford. Preferably these should incorporate ear defenders to eliminate outside background noise. It is no good receiving a signal you can't analyse due to poor quality headphones – after all, it would be a shame to miss that Saxon gold coin, wouldn't it? (For further information on headphones see Chapter 6.)

Before you even start to assemble the detector you have bought, read the instruction book and follow the advice it gives on how to do this. Adjust the shaft length to suit your height and reach. It is most important that you feel comfortable. Your arm should be straight and relaxed; if the shaft is set too short you will be detecting with your back bent, which will result in back

*Before you unpack your new detector always study the instructions. (Whites Electronics (UK) Ltd and Minelab International Ltd)*

OPPOSITE: *Correct adjustment of the shaft is most important. This detectorist appears to be comfortable with his machine.*

pain. Remember that as you extend the shaft you increase the strain on your wrist and arm due to the increased leverage. Overextending the shaft will mean that you will be detecting with your arm bent, which will put a strain on your elbow and shoulder.

Put the batteries in and set up the controls, following the instructions. It is really important that you familiarize yourself with every aspect of your detector. Complaints are often heard that a certain type of detector is bad or difficult, yet when help and advice is offered the novice detectorist starts saying thing like 'I didn't realize it did that', 'I didn't know you could adjust it to do that' or 'Where did you find all that information?' Nine times out of ten the answer is in the machine's instruction manual.

A similar situation used to arise when I was producing turbocharger conversion kits for Land Rovers and various tractors. We received so many enquiries from customers who had failed to read the instructions properly, if at all, that one of my staff came up with the brilliant idea of printing the following text on the packing cases in large clear lettering: 'When all else fails, read the instructions'.

I cannot emphasize enough what good advice this is. Remember that it relates to all makes and models of metal detectors.

One group of detectorists who often don't follow the instructions are those who have been detecting for some time and then part exchange or purchase a new machine of a similar type to their existing one. The detector may have had good reviews in the detecting magazines, but unless the instructions and techniques of using it are followed the best performance will not be achieved. It's no good thinking 'I know this type of detector, I've been using a similar one for ages'. Technology moves on and all makes and

*Test samples.*

models need to be learnt and practised with to attain the best results.

The next step is to practise using the controls and display the detector has to identify metals and artefacts of different types and shapes. For this you will need to gather together a range of sample items:

- Some iron screws or nails.
- A ring-pull from a drinks can.
- A selection of coins.
- Tinfoil.
- A silver ring and medallion.
- A gold ring and medallion.
- A silver or gold chain.

*Camouflaged test coins.*

## AIR DETECTING PRACTISE

Now we can start to use the detector. First place the detector on a wooden table with the search coil at 90 degrees to the stem and at least 1m away from any metal objects such as radiators, concrete floor reinforcing bars or bolts in the table. Then, following your detector's instruction manual, switch on and set it up to start detecting.

To ensure that you don't receive any false signals, remove any jewellery, watch, belt buckle or cufflinks you may be wearing. Take each sample item in turn and pass it backwards and forwards across the face of the coil, noting the difference in sound between each item. After a while your ear will become more used to the individual sound each item gives. Make a list of the items and alongside each write a description of the sound it makes in a way that you can understand. Don't worry about anyone else understanding it: someone I know swears that his detector gives a shrill, high-pitched 'Yes' when it's a good signal and a deep, low-pitched 'Don't' when it's a junk signal. It really doesn't matter

what anyone else thinks of your description, as long as you recognize and interpret that signal correctly every time it occurs.

Now put the same items into individual envelopes or waterproof opaque bags, number them and record their numbers against the items on your written list. This will mean you are unable to see the individual items. Then repeat the previous exercise.

As you progress, you can add another level of difficulty into the practice exercises. When you feel more confident, ask someone to pass the numbered packets across the face of the coil so you can guess what the contents are. Put on your headphones and listen carefully to the individual sound each item makes. Then make a record of their distinctive description and what you think the item is. After each practice run you can check how you have done with your friend. In order to make this exercise even more testing and to further hone your skills, try wearing a blindfold.

The next exercise is to take the sealed envelopes out into the garden or to a local field. Place them on the ground in a line, approximately

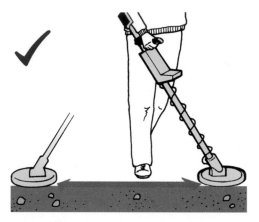 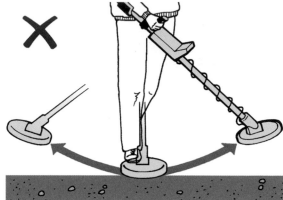

*The right and wrong way to swing the detector.*

1m apart, with the written number face down. Following the maker's instructions, switch on and adjust the setting for your detector. Just before you begin, try to hold the memory of each item's distinct sound in your mind. You can now start to search for the items using the following methods. The sounds your detector makes as it passes over different objects are much like a foreign language that you need to learn. At first your interpretation will be rather similar to the attempts at 'French' made by Officer Crabtree in the TV comedy *'Allo, 'Allo*. With practice and perseverance, however, your comprehension of the detector's language will improve and the number and quality of your finds will increase accordingly (see Appendix four).

Even experienced detectorists find it useful to spend some time air testing to get their ears 'tuned in' to the different range of signals that will be encountered when, for example, they will be searching for Euro coins rather than British currency.

After at least a couple of days of air test practise and gaining experience, you should be ready to start working on search techniques.

## GROUND DETECTING PRACTICE

One of the hardest techniques to master when using a metal detector in the field, and yet probably the most important to acquire, is the overlapping sweeping motion used to search the ground and ensure the fullest possible coverage of the search area. On a piece of flat ground swing the detector back and forth as if you were detecting and determine the actual width of your swing. A person who is 1.8m tall, for example, will have a swing of approximately 2m. Using a detector with an 18cm diameter coil, the detector will need to be swung from side to side eleven times for every 2m advanced in order to cover the ground completely. When out detecting, however, you will normally be advancing more rapidly, so you must always remember that you are only sampling the ground and not covering it 100 per cent.

To achieve the maximum depth during the search it is vital that the coil head is kept parallel to and as close to the ground as possible throughout the whole of the side-to-side swing. This may sound easy but it takes a lot of concentration and practise to get it right consistently.

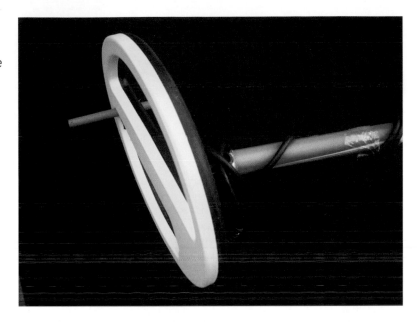

*A marker fixed to the coil and protruding about 5cm. This will leave a line on the ground to show the path of the coil during the sweep.*

There is, for example, a common tendency to lift the coil at the end of each sweep.

The speed of the swing is another factor that must be controlled: too fast and you will miss signals, too slow and the detector will struggle to work properly. Remember that this is a *motion* detector. The correct duration of a sweep will be about two seconds each way, depending on the length of the arc being used.

The following exercise will show you whether you are doing the sweep correctly or whether you need more practice. Even the most experienced detectorist will benefit from practising it since it can be very easy to slip into bad habits over the years. First take your detector and a lollypop stick, or something similar that is non-metallic. Fasten it to the coil of your detector, using insulating tape, so that 5cm protrudes below the coil face towards the ground. Now start your sweep pattern over smooth soil or on a sandy beach. Walk slowly forwards, ensuring the stick is marking a line in the sand all the way through the arc. Look at the relationship between your footprints and the arcs of your swing. Even very experienced detectorists will be surprised at how little of the ground covered has actually been searched. This is even more important if your detector has a concentric coil, which emits a conical-shaped signal, rather than the greater coverage provided by the rectangular signal pattern emitted by a doubled 'D' type coil, as used by some manufacturers. At a depth of 20cm, for example, a concentric coil may search as little as 20mm in diameter.

## SEARCH PATTERNS

Having learned the correct way to use the detector, you will want to get started. First, however, there are one or two more nuggets of knowledge to pass on. When you arrive at your field take a few moments to study the lie of the land. Are there any unnatural features? Depressions can equal moats or ditches. Humps and straight lines could indicate buildings. Changes in the colour of the soil could be fires or aircraft crash

*Not all of the ground is actually searched. Walking too quickly and swinging too slowly will leave large amounts of ground undetected. The correct swing of the detector is of vital importance.*

sites. These are but a few of the possibilities that could offer an indication of any previous occupation of the site. You next need to establish which of the possible search patterns should be adopted when searching the field.

### Lonely Slug

The first pattern you might choose to adopt is the random or 'lonely slug' search pattern, in which you wander where the mood takes you. Arguments in favour of this search pattern might be that it's a relaxed pattern to follow – after all, detecting should be fun – and you can go over to talk to friends whenever you like, since you wouldn't be breaking a rigid search pattern that you can't pick up again. Some people who follow this type of search pattern occasionally find things and they still enjoy the hobby, but it should be remembered that if artefacts in a given field are distributed at random, the chances of finding them are reduced if you do not carry out a systematic search.

### Envelope Search

The second search pattern you might consider is the 'envelope search' pattern. If you turn a small envelope over and look at the back you will see what I mean. Taking a near square field as our example, detect all the way around the field and then detect across the diagonals. This is the search pattern I habitually use when detecting on a site for the first time, unless I have been told of hotspots (areas that have a concentration of finds). To start the envelope search in a field, take four paces in towards the centre of the field from the fence or hedgerow and then set off round the field. The reason I would suggest four paces is that I know of a case where a small hoard was found in just such a position. It also seems the sort of distance from a hedge where a ploughman with a team of horses would have started walking and therefore had the greatest chance of losing any items from his pockets. After this, search across the two diagonals.

This search pattern might be predictable, but you will discover that it helps to build up a picture of what you can expect to find when you return to the field a second or third time. It will also show where finds are more clearly as you work your way round the four triangles of the field. What you are trying to do is find any hotspots that there might be in the field. These need not be large, or obvious, so keep your eyes open for clues such as pieces of pottery or flint artefacts as well as the signals from your detector. The information on 'eyes only' searching (Appendix Three) should help if you are trying to make sense of such finds. The arguments against this type of search pattern might be that it can be boring and predictable, or leave you a

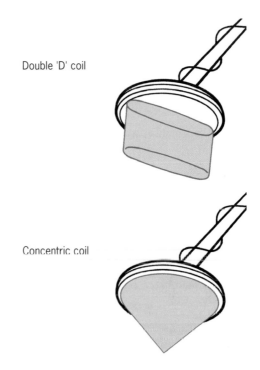

Double 'D' coil

Concentric coil

*The shape of the signal emitted by the two types of coil.*

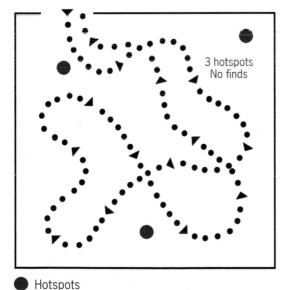

3 hotspots
No finds

● Hotspots

*'Lonely slug' random search pattern.*

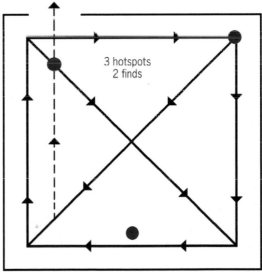

3 hotspots
2 finds

● Hotspots

*Envelope search pattern.*

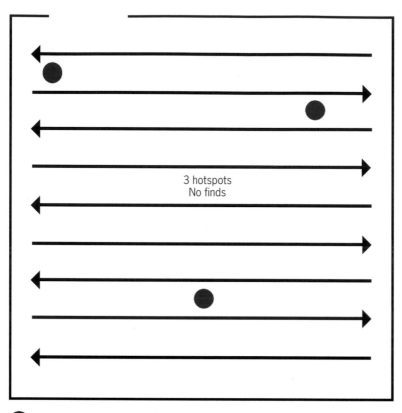

*Gridiron search pattern.*

3 hotspots
No finds

● Hotspots

long way from your friends should they make a nice find and you want to pop over to look at it.

### Gridiron Search

I would recommend that you adopt the 'gridiron' search pattern as soon as you think you have found a hotspot or an area rich in human activity. In this pattern you cross the area back and forth along parallel lines set as far apart as the distance you swing your detector side to side, which as was stated above would be about 2m for someone who is 1.8m tall.

Since you are in a field and not measuring it on paper with a ruler, the methods used to set out a gridiron search pattern need to be consistent rather than inch-perfect.

The method will require two 'find markers', which can be as simple as fluorescent tape wrapped around a wire peg. Firstly put your spade in the ground and walk three or four paces at right angles to the direction you intend to detect. Insert the first peg into the ground, with the tape tied to it. Then return to the spade, fix on a point in the hedge across the field and work towards it while detecting. Once you have reached the far side of the site, you now need to detect back to the first marker peg. Once again take three or four paces at right angles to your search direction and place the spade in the ground. Then move on a further three or four paces and put the second marker peg and fluorescent tape in the ground. Go back to the spade and detect across the field towards the first marker peg. You will find that it is simpler to do than to describe.

We know that a swing covers only 2m, yet the rows on the gridiron pattern are three or four paces apart, so we must accept that this method will only sample the area. You will also find that your lines will probably not be as straight as they might be. A handy tip, when you are detecting on ploughed fields, is to follow the plough or harrow lines. You can also distance yourself by watching your footprints in the soil from the previous search line. For more detailed coverage of an area you can close up your grid lines and progress with overlapping swings. The choice is yours, but just be aware of the difference between sampling and a complete search of the ground you are covering.

Every detectorist has his or her preferred means of working, but sometimes a change can lead to a surprising result. The following true story happened when Tim and Andy (not their real names) were detecting together at a rally. Tim habitually detects using the 'lonely slug' search pattern, while Andy is highly methodical and uses the gridiron pattern whenever possible. That day Andy was trying to get Tim to mend his ways and pay more attention to making his technique more systematic. Tim has a great deal of experience and has found a significant number of coins and artefacts, so he probably didn't think his searching style needed improving. As the two friends continued detecting together they eventually reached a spot where Andy was finding Roman pottery. Reluctantly Tim complied

*Marker peg kit.*

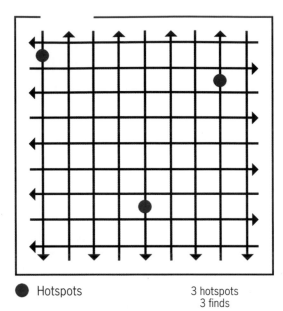

● Hotspots                           3 hotspots
                                     3 finds

*Double gridiron search pattern.*

### Double Gridiron

The fourth technique you might choose to adopt is the 'double gridiron' pattern. This consists of overlaying the first gridiron pattern on a second at right angles to the first.

My wife regularly uses the double gridiron pattern on sites, since she finds it so effective, but it is still not the last word. Sometimes I have joined her after she has completed her double grid search for a final pass across the site. We then do a 'diagonal gridiron' search, just to see if anything is left, by detecting across the diagonals of the square from opposite directions. In effect this means carrying out an 'envelope pattern' search over the top of a double gridiron pattern. We have learned that, while the double gridiron pattern is effective, it still doesn't find everything. Both of us have made further useful finds on sites where we have applied the diagonal gridiron search pattern after the conventional double gridiron search. This only reinforces what I have said before: *most of the time we are only sampling the ground.*

with Andy's wishes to get his act together and search more methodically. The end of the story was predictable: it was Tim, and not Andy, who turned up the Celtic gold stater coin. I heard this story from 'Andy' and he was genuinely pleased that his friend had been successful through following his instructions. I am sure that, with his attention to detail and methodical search techniques, Andy will turn up something of similar value in the near future. It would be interesting to know whether the experience has changed Tim's search strategy.

> **The more you practise,
> the luckier you get.
> Learn the language
> of your detector.**

# CHAPTER 5

# IDENTIFICATION AND RECOVERY OF TARGETS

Once you are able to tune in your detector and know how to cover a search area methodically, you are ready to move on to the next stage. When you have located a target, listen carefully to the signal and decide if it is of a type and quality worth further investigation and recovery. If so, you must now learn how to get the artefact out of the ground safely without damaging it.

Before we start to dig, however, our detector can help give us a much clearer impression of what lies beneath the surface, for example how deep it is buried, what kind of shape it may be and what kind of metal it is composed of.

A metal detector works by reading the differences in the magnetic field below it, so each different type of metal produces its own individual signal. Learning these signals will improve your enjoyment and make your detecting much more efficient.

The strength of the signal can tell us two things: the size of the target and its depth. Only dedicated practice and experience can teach you the differences, but it is worth learning to decipher them. Every make of machine will handle these differently, so it is important to study the maker's manual and then practise.

The electronics in the detector can help us determine the shape of our find and its exact position. You will have found the signal by slowly walking forward and swinging the detector from side to side in a steady flat arc. By moving the detector repeatedly side to side over the target, you can hold in your mind the spot where the signal is strongest. The target, however, could be anywhere across the diameter of the coil, so turn through 90 degrees and repeat the sweep across the target. This should give you a point where the two sweeps of the detector cross on the ground. The target lays where the signal is strongest in both directions. This process is known as 'pinpointing'.

Some machines incorporate a visual pinpoint facility, which, when activated, effectively turns the detector into a TR machine. The detector does not have to be moved to generate a signal, but instead produces its strongest signal when the target is directly beneath the centre of the coil. On some detectors this pinpointing is included in the visual display.

To summarize, once we have a target signal we can know exactly where it's located and, by the strength of the signal, we may be able to tell how deep it is in the ground (the stronger signals will be shallow, weak signals will be deeper ones). Finally we know from the tone what metal it may be made of.

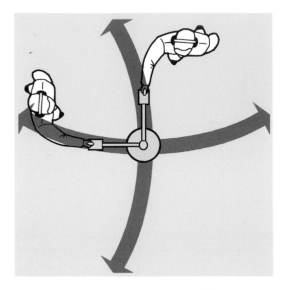

*Pinpointing by crossing the swings of the detector.*

One last bit of wizardry the detector can do for us is to help identify what shape the target might be:

- A coin gives a sharp, clear signal.
- A ring gives a double signal.
- A nail or spike gives a repeated signal along its length, but a single signal across its width.
- A chain or bracelet often gives a repeated signal in both directions.
- Tinfoil often gives a spluttering or crackling signal.

It is important to learn what shape the target may be since, to put it simply, this knowledge might prevent you from damaging an article that may be of immense historic value. If, on the other hand, it should prove to be a piece of modern jewellery, its monetary value could

*The circle on the right of the screen is complete when the target is pinpointed.*

be dramatically reduced if irreparably damaged. From personal experience I know what damage can be done if you do not dig accurately.

You should now be in a position to appreciate why it is so important to practise with your detector. Learn its language. It is continually giving you information that, if you can decipher it, should help you find and safely recover interesting and possibly valuable artefacts.

## REMOVING THE ARTICLE FROM THE GROUND

Having established the precise location of the artefact, it is now time to remove it from the ground and recover it. In my experience the safest means is to remove a small plug of ground that contains the artefact. For small objects, cut three sides of a 15cm cube around the artefact using a small stainless-steel recovery spade or a diver's knife. Cutting a hinged plug will ensure that it is returned to the correct place and also reduces the chance of damaging the find.

Scan the plug and the hole with the detector or, if you have one, a handheld pinpoint detector. If the artefact is in the plug, you should be able to locate it by careful probing with a knife or screwdriver. If the artefact remains in the hole

*Inaccurate recovery can cause damage, as shown on this gold ring, which was not the author's most successful find.*

you may have to remove more soil, each time repeating the scanning process by passing a handful of recovered soil across the detector's coil until the find is safely located. Make sure you do not have any rings or metal items on your hands or wrists.

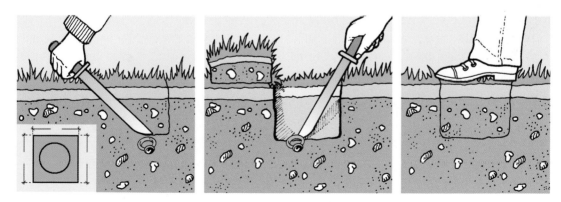

*The recovery process using a knife or chisel. The procedure is the same if using a spade.*

*Scan every handful of soil removed from the hole until you recover the target.*

Make a further search of the area for additional signals. There have been cases of up to fourteen coins being found in and around a single hole by repeatedly scanning the hole and the spoil, so don't get carried away with the excitement of the first find.

It is very important to look after the environment by making only a small hole and then replacing the sand, soil or turf as neatly as possible. It is essential for the good name of the hobby that you do not leave a field or beach looking like a First World War battlefield. Should you find you have recovered an item that is rubbish (or what most detectorists prefer to call junk), always take it with you and dispose of it responsibly in the appropriate recycling bin.

An important word of warning is needed at this stage. Never detect without gloves of some kind. The actual type is up to each individual, but they should be 'fit for purpose' and provide protection from sharp articles. Some of the best have Kevlar, the materiel from which police stab vests are made, on the inner fingers and the area of the palm. Always be aware there can be some very unpleasant things lurking both on and in the ground, ranging from chemicals to germs, and from old nails to broken glass. A cut hand is not the best way to find them. (For further details on this subject, see Chapter 7.)

## RECOVERY TOOLS

You may already have some of the tools that can be used for recovering the artefacts that we locate around your house or in the garden shed, but others are more specialized. Many detectorists develop their own preference for digging tools. The following list, with some of their uses, is presented in no particular order:

- Gardener's hand trowel or hoe, used to recover items in soft sand or soil.
- Gardener's hand rake, used to recover items from a stony surface or a shingle beach.
- Sheath knife or diver's knife, used to cut out a small sod of grass and soil, and making possible a very neat recovery.
- A strong, long screwdriver, useful as a probe.
- A lady's small gardening spade. This can be used in many detecting conditions, but make sure it's not too heavy, since even a light one will feel quite heavy after carrying it for two or three hours.
- A lady's small garden fork, useful on ploughed fields or heavy ground.

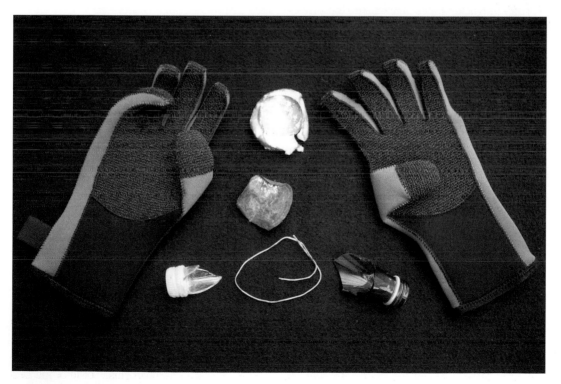

*Kevlar-faced gloves are recommended when dealing with sharp pieces of junk.*

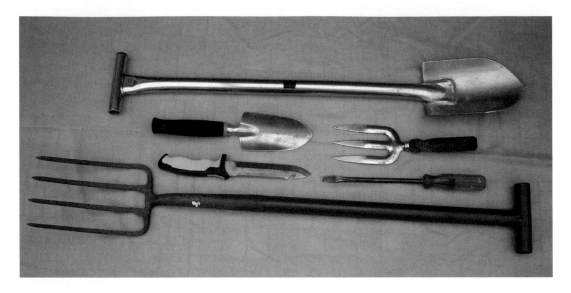

*A selection of recovery tools.*

There are also ranges of specialist tools available from companies such as Black Adder. These may be bought from local metal-detecting dealers or from advertisements in the detecting magazines.

## TAKING CARE OF YOUR DETECTOR

If by now you have used your detector out in the field, and perhaps have even made your first find, do not go home and just leave it in a cupboard. Follow the simple advice on looking after your machine that you may already have read in the instruction book. It would do no harm, however, to run through the do's and don'ts of caring for a detector.

Taking care of your detector is mostly common sense. All detectors are complex electronic instruments that have required extensive research in their design and development. Manufacturers will have taken into account the environment in which they will be used, but they also need a little help and tender loving care from the owner. A few general points apply to all types and makes of machines:

- Avoid rapid changes in temperature. Large temperature swings can create condensation inside the machine, which could damage the electronics.
- Never leave the machine in direct hot sunshine as the temperatures of the coil and the control box could easily reach 60 or 70 degrees Celsius, which again could damage the electronics.
- After using the machine always clean off any mud, soil or sand with a moist cloth or soft brush. Wipe it over with a cloth dampened with a little WD40. Then undo the plugs to the control box and give them a clean with WD40.
- Remove the coil cover and clean both the coil and the cover with a moist cloth. This is especially important if you have been beach or water detecting since fine

sand and silt will get in between the coil and its cover. This condition can produce ghost signals or, even worse, mask out signals altogether, so causing us to miss that gold coin or ring.

■ Always remove the batteries if you are not planning to use your detector for a few days. This prevents corrosion that could ruin your machine. If you do remove the batteries, store them somewhere warm such as an airing cupboard. This helps the batteries to recover and they will perform better when you go to use them the next time.

■ Never pull or tug at the leads, since it can damage the wiring and produce erratic signals.

As you make your first steps in metal detecting, you may find yourself mixing with experienced

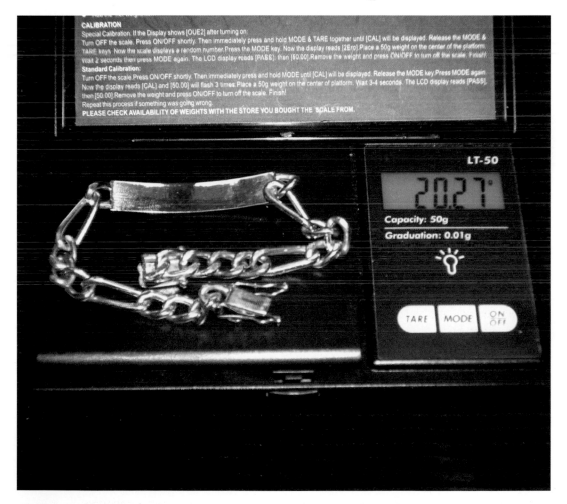

*A gold bracelet found on a beach that had already been 'done'. Remember that we are only sampling when we search.*

## SIMPLE TROUBLESHOOTING GUIDE

**No sound**

- Check batteries are fitted correctly.
- Check batteries are fully charged.
- Check the detector is switched on.
- Check headphone lead.

**Inconsistent signals**

- Check batteries are fully charged.
- Check headphone lead.
- Reduce the sensitivity setting.
- Check for sand and grit between the coil and its cover.
- Check for overhead electricity wires or cables.
- Check that no mobile phones are switched on close to your detector.
- Move away from any other detectorists working close to you.
- If none of these corrects the fault, contact your dealer. Do not open up the machine as this may invalidate any warranty and could cause further damage.

detectorists who seem to have all the luck. Don't become disheartened, but keep plugging away at it. Watch them, copy their good habits, reject their bad ones and, above all, keep practising.

Towards the end of my first year of detecting I found a 20 gram gold bracelet on a beach in Spain. It was by far my best find at the time. I had been staying at the beach for a few days, during which I had probably spent about eight to ten hours detecting. A local man who came to the beach with a detector every evening tried to put me off by claiming it was 'his beach' – and anyway there was nothing left as he had done it all. As the photograph on the previous page shows, that was not the case.

> **Keep searching and stay optimistic. Remember, nobody gets it all.**

# CHAPTER 6

# SAFETY FIRST

## THE WEATHER AND THE ENVIRONMENT

I am constantly amazed at the scant observation of safety procedures by many people involved in outdoor pursuits, including metal detecting. A good starting point for the rules on safety is the Countryside Code, available from the Ramblers' Association (www.ramblers.org.uk/info/britain/countrysidecode.htm).

Never underestimate the environment you are in, as the circumstances and the weather can change very quickly. It is so easy, even in summer, to be caught in a sudden squall or rainstorm. When the wind-chill factor is taken into account, the effective temperature can drop rapidly. A mild, pleasant spring or early summer's day temperature of perhaps 18 to 20 degrees can plunge in a freak rainstorm and become effectively close to zero when the wind-chill factor is taken into consideration. These are not the conditions in which to be caught wearing only tee shirt and shorts. Be prepared. Always carry a spare set of dry clothes in your car.

These are also the conditions where thunder and lightening can be present, so you should be particularly careful since your detector and spade will both contain metal. Modern detectors also contain carbon fibre, which is another excellent conductor. Do get an up-to-date weather forecast for the local area where you going to detect. The most detailed should be available from the control tower at an airfield close to where your detecting site, if you are detecting inland, or from the coast guard for conditions on the coast or near the sea. A general forecast from the radio or television does not contain enough detail.

A recent detecting trip to northern Spain supplies an example of how quickly conditions can change. The forecast given on the Internet stated that the Burgos area would be expecting heavy showers but bright periods and a chance of a cold spell for the next few days. When we disembarked at Santander it was indeed bright but cold.

During the journey south towards Burgos, however, it became apparent that detecting might be difficult: overnight there had been a heavy fall of snow and the intended site was now under nearly a metre.

I had done my research at home using the Internet weather sites, but that had been two days earlier and the sites did not have sufficient detail. In short, it was just not good enough. At least this mistake did not have any dangerous consequences.

## BASIC SAFETY

The following is not an exhaustive list of warnings and procedures, but provides a basic starting point for what needs to considered whenever you go out detecting, whether for an hour, a day or longer.

First, follow the recommendations given for walking groups, which have been tried and tested over many years. Make sure that you leave behind a detailed plan, either at home or at least visible in your parked car. This should contain accurate listings of the map reference or GPS (global positioning system) coordinates of all the sites you plan to be visiting during your search, together with the time you expect to arrive at and depart from each of the sites. Indicate any distinctive coloured clothing or items that would quickly highlight your whereabouts on a site, such as fluorescent jackets, dayglo hats or backpacks. Make sure that the numbers of all the mobile phones that will be with the party are recorded on the list in case you find yourself out of range or the phone is switched off; in that way your friends at base should still be able to make contact with the group.

## Buddy System

This system really is very simple: do not go out without a 'buddy'. Always have a plan prepared for your time out, so that both of you know what the other is going to be doing and in what area. Stay within easy contact distance – certainly within sight – and have an agreed time to make contact with a wave, say every 15 minutes. You should also have a simple code, such as one hand waved for 'OK' and two hands waved for 'I need you now' (plus, of course, the standard sign for 'It's time for a cup of tea').

*On even the finest day the weather can change very quickly.*

*A one-handed wave for 'OK', two hands for 'I need you now'.*

There are several reasons for this system:

- Help will be on hand in case you should have an accident, break a leg or have any serious medical problems.
- This system provides security, especially important for the young or women.
- You will be assured of a helping hand in the event that you become entangled in barbed wire or have a similar problem
- Should you be taking children with you, make sure you have one adult per child, or one adult who can be a non-detecting childminder.
- By having a 'buddy' with you, you also are able to witness each other's finds and actions. (This could be helpful should you find something of archaeological importance or high value.)
- There is nothing like sharing the experience of a really good find with a friend.

### Warm-up and Cool-down Exercises

As with any sport or energetic hobby, it is prudent to warm your muscles up before starting any exercise. Further, when the session out in the field, on the beach or in the water is completed, it is wise to give muscles some cooling down stretches and exercises. Be aware that detecting sessions can often last for four or five hours and can involve a lot of bending and digging.

The exercises on the following pages were devised for me by a fitness instructor after I developed a stiff case of 'detectorist's shoulder' on the right-hand side, probably caused by too much detecting. I have no doubt that these exercises have been most helpful, although I felt a bit conspicuous when I first tried them. I've also shared these techniques with fellow detectorists, and there is now a growing number who can vouch for the benefits of following a regime of stretches before and after detecting.

*Warm-up and cool-down exercises suitable for hobbies such as metal detecting. (Kyrie Davis)*

(a) Hamstring stretch. Feet hip distance apart. Step one foot forward. Bend knee on the back leg and place hands on top of thigh of bent leg. Bend forwards from hips and slide hands down the thigh until stretch is felt in back of straight leg.

(b) Quadriceps stretch. Balance on one leg. Raise heel of opposite leg towards buttock cheek. Feel stretch in front of thigh on the bent leg.

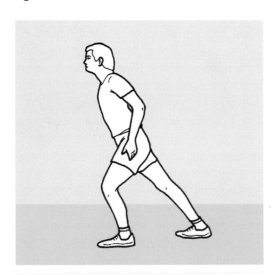

(c) Calf stretch. Start with feet hip distance apart. Step right leg back as far as possible but keep heel of back foot on floor. Feel stretch in back of shin on back leg.

(d) Back of the upper arm stretch. Stand with feet hip distance apart. Place one hand in the centre of the back and use other arm to ease the arm further back.

(e) Chest stretch. Start with feet hip distance apart. Take hands backwards until a mild tension is felt in front of the chest.

(f) Middle back stretch. Stand with feet shoulder width and a half apart. Take both arms forwards in front of the body just below shoulder height and link the fingers. Round the shoulders slightly to feel mild tension in the middle of the upper back.

(g) Bicep curl. Keeping elbows pressed into sides of the body, raise forearms and curl hands towards shoulders. Return arms without locking elbows.

(h) Breast stroke. Move arms in a breast stroke swimming action in front of the body. Keep shoulders relaxed and elbows unlocked.

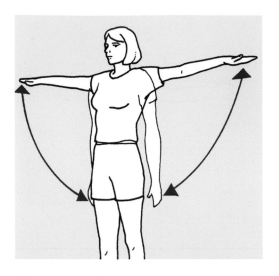

*(i) Lateral raise. Start with arms at the side of the body, raise arms sideways until they are level with the shoulders. Keep the elbows unlocked and shoulders relaxed.*

*(j) Shoulder press. Start with arms bent and hands level with shoulders. Extend arms above head and return to start position.*

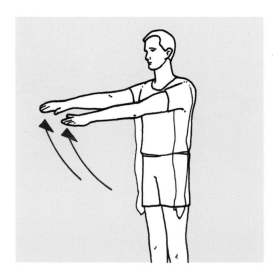

*(k) Front raise. Start with arms by side of body. Raise arms slightly in front of body to shoulder height. Keep elbows slightly bent.*

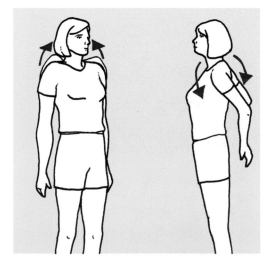

*(l) Shoulder lifts and rolls. Stand with feet hip distance apart. Shoulder lifts – lift shoulders towards ears. Shoulder rolls – roll shoulders backwards and then forwards.*

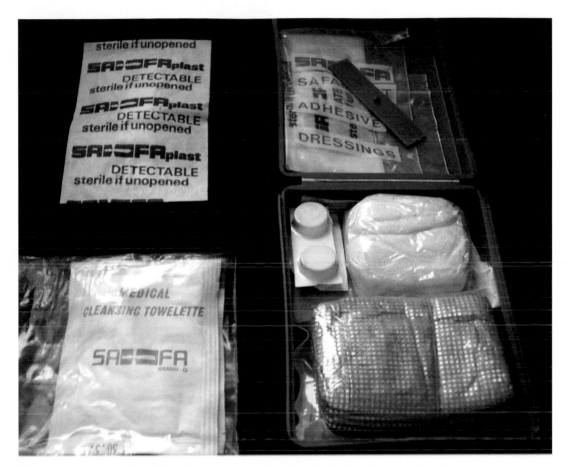

*Always carry a basic first aid kit. A more comprehensive kit should be kept back in the car.*

### First Aid Kit

The kit you carry with you does not need to be that extensive, as you can always leave a more comprehensive selection of items in your car. I would suggest that you should always have the following to hand:

- wound dressing
- sterile lint pack
- sticking plasters
- sting/bite ointment
- bottle of antiseptic hand or wound wash

I have found that St John Ambulance has always been helpful in providing advice concerning what to have in your kit and supplying information booklets on what to do in an emergency (available at www.sja.org.uk/sja/first-aid-advice. aspx).

### Mobile Phone

This may seem a rather obvious item to mention nowadays, but mobile phones are included here because people have been known to have various problems with them, both technical (flat battery or not enough credit on the card) and personal ('I left it in the car' or 'I can't remember the pin number'). It is a good idea to have all the relevant emergency numbers ready loaded into your phone as speed-dial numbers. Save your partner's number to be used as ICE (In Case of Emergency). If you are going to detect on the beach or in the water, it is prudent to include the Coast Guard in your list of speed-dialled numbers. Calling them direct can save a few precious minutes in an emergency involving a rising tide.

### Tetanus Injections and Medication

Your local doctor should be able to confirm whether you have had a tetanus injection and whether the booster jabs are up to date. This is essential since you will be digging in ground that may have had agricultural chemicals spread on it, or it may be contaminated in some other way. There is also the chance of objects such as nails, screws, pieces of metal and old knives being buried in the soil or sand. I have seen some pretty gruesome injuries caused by a sloppy attitude to junk, and I cannot emphasize too strongly the need to take care.

When away detecting you should also make sure that you have any prescription medication, pills or 'puffers' that you or anyone in your group may need during the trip.

### Additional Accessories

Over the years I have gathered a collection of items that have been useful in various circumstances. When all the detectorists in a group are

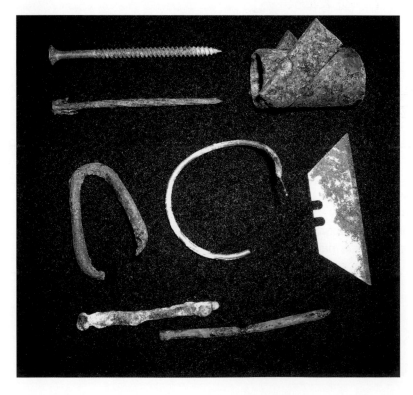

*There can be very nasty things below the surface, so always take care.*

*A couple of items that can be really useful on occasion, notably a whistle.*

wearing headphones, for example, it can be difficult to hear a shout, so a piercing police whistle can help draw their attention. It is also amazing how many things can be fixed using a Swiss Army knife or similar pocket tool, so avoiding a trip back to the car.

It is useful to put together an emergency repair kit to deal with minor technical problems. This should include a roll of insulating tape, which can be wound round the body of a miniature LED torch in order to help direct the light when it starts to get dark. A coil of 3mm fencing wire, about 50cm long, and a length of dayglo tape, of the type used for road works, can be used to make a marker flag for your detecting pattern or for marking an important or dangerous find. You could also have spare parts for your machine, such as a plastic nut, bolt and washers for the detector coil and spare batteries.

I am not suggesting that you must take all of these, but experience has shown that each could be of value in certain circumstances. As you gain experience you will find what should be included in a kit to suit your own needs.

## SAFETY DURING THE RECOVERY OF ITEMS

### Holes

Do not get carried away digging deep holes. They can be dangerous. In addition, you should remember that your detector is unlikely to find quality items any deeper than about 30 to 40cm. If you are still receiving a signal at this depth it is likely to be something like a ploughshare or even larger, so leave it. After you have retrieved the item always remember to fill in your holes; it is inconsiderate to fail to do so, as well as dangerous to farm workers, walkers or other detectorists.

### Junk Pouches

During a detecting session you may have found all manner of unpleasant bits and pieces and stuffed them in your junk pouch. Always wear gloves when putting your hand into the pouch. It is all too easy to forget what has already gone

*More bits and pieces that have proved useful out in the field – including a mini torch and some detector spares (bolts, washers, brackets, batteries, etc.).*

in there and is now hidden in the dark. I know of people who have suffered serious injury from one small lapse of concentration. This is something that could be avoided with a little forethought and good gloves such as those illustrated in the previous chapter.

*A fine example of a restored pistol.*

## Munitions and Weapons

Guns, knives and swords are rare finds, although they do turn up now and again, usually in a state of corrosion. Be very careful if you unearth anything like this. It is indeed better to leave it where it is and to call the archaeologists (via the local museum) and/or the police. This could also be an excellent opportunity to build positive relations with both of these local organizations.

You should be aware that the act of taking weapons of any kind away from the site may well put you foul of the law. There are very strict rules covering the possession of weapons and firearms; knives and swords are covered by similar rules. If you would like to keep the find, inform the police at the time you call them to the site. Following their investigation, they will inform you of the weapon's status. If it could possibly be classed as an antique, you may be permitted to keep the find and restore it. Even if is not classified as an antique weapon, you may

*Should you ever find something like this mortar bomb, do not touch it: call 999 and follow instructions.*

*This Spanish valley cannot be used for arable farming due to the amount of unexploded munitions left over from the Spanish Civil War over 70 years ago. Clearance is continually taking place.*

be allowed to keep it after you have paid for it to be deactivated by an approved gunsmith. If this is the case, make sure that you acquire the correct certificate to confirm that it is legal for you to own the weapon and keep it at home.

Munitions and ammunition are also rare finds. If you ever find anything that looks even remotely like a bomb, a mortar round or something similar – or even a bullet or shell from a gun – *do not touch it*! You must immediately use something to mark the spot clearly, such as a marker flag. Then make your retreat by walking slowly backwards, keeping eye contact with the marker. Once you are well clear, use your whistle to get the rest of your group's attention. Make sure they also withdraw from the site and do not take a route that brings them close to the suspect find. When you have accounted for everyone, call the police or bomb disposal team.

Mount guard on the site to prevent any walkers or farmworkers approaching the dangerous find. If you are on a remote site away from the nearest road, arrange for someone to meet the police at the nearest access point to the site and act as a guide. (This is another good reason for using the 'buddy' system.)

For information on safety measures to be observed on beaches, in estuaries and in the water, see Chapters 13 and 14.

> Metal detecting is an exciting hobby
> and we can get carried away.
> Make sure you are the one who
> walks away from it.
> Safety first, finds second.

*Bullets and shell cases should be treated with extreme caution.*

# CHAPTER 7

# CLOTHING AND ANCILLARY EQUIPMENT

Metal detecting is a hobby of extremes. Some detectorists travel great distances, even going abroad, for the chance to detect on a choice site. They use incredibly sophisticated computer-controlled metal detectors and put enormous effort into research and cleaning their finds. Yet you can regularly see detectorists wearing old army clothing, jeans and trainers – indeed sometimes it looks as though they've put on anything that came to hand.

Every other hobby or leisure activity seems to have developed a 'complete package' when it comes to clothing and equipment. Can you imagine a racing driver wearing other than

*These people are demonstrating how not to go about detecting. One of them has no headphones and they have no recovery tools, no gloves and the detectors are being waved about all over the place.*

purpose-made fireproof clothing? Would a climber wear inappropriate clothing and boots when setting off for a day's climbing? Even walkers and ramblers invest in purpose-made equipment, including boots and suitable clothing. Perhaps we can learn from these other activities.

*A well-equipped walker and his kit. (Richard Gosnell)*

## BASIC ADVICE FOR WALKERS AND RAMBLERS

*(with thanks to Richard Gosnell)*

When out walking, always walk with a companion, since aggressive farmers are less likely to cause problems if you are not alone. This also applies to aggressive dogs. If you encounter trouble one of you can make a phone call for help while the other is dealing with the problem. The following list is the minimum that you should carry to deal with most eventualities:

- Rucksack
- Stout boots
- Water
- Penknife
- Secateurs (useful for snipping brambles and similar nuisances)
- First aid kit
- Mobile phone (always check that it is charged)
- GPS unit (and spare batteries)
- Magnetic compass
- Map and waterproof map case

# CLOTHING

A brief description can cover only a few of the many possibilities available to those seeking high-quality clothing for outdoor activities. I shall start at the top and work down.

**Headwear.** A hat should have long peak to keep out any glare from the sun. It should be light or bright in colour, and preferably dayglo. This can help in locating you should you get into difficulties. In a hot climate you might consider a cap with an additional neck cover to avoid sunburn. A fleece tube neck warmer can help keep you warm in winter.

Few detectorists set out when it is raining, but if you do you will need a hat or cap of similar style but waterproof. Gun shops are an excellent source of 'high visibility' dayglo hats, skeet vests and other items of clothing intended for beaters, and these often have the advantage of being waterproof.

**Underclothing.** In winter you will want something made from a high-performance fabric that helps keep you warm. Look for natural fibres like silk and for designs that 'wick' away the moisture from perspiration.

**Outer clothing.** This should be suited to the season. In summer lightweight natural cotton materials take a lot of beating. In winter or cold weather some of the higher performance outdoor clothing made from modern materials

*Wearing a high visibility cap and vest means that a detectorist can easily be seen. This also gives a more 'official' appearance when on site and in the public eye.*

like Gore-Tex is excellent, although it can be expensive. A good range of performance clothing at a price suited to more restricted budgets can be found in builders' merchants or industrial workwear suppliers. Their comprehensive clothing ranges are made for tough environments and may have extra padding where it is needed, for example on the knees and the seat areas of the trousers. They sometimes also have the advantage of a generous cut to allow for bending and stretching. The reflective safety strips that are often fitted on the legs and jackets can be useful in an emergency should it be getting dark.

**Rainwear.** I would not recommend detecting in the rain since few detectors for use inland are waterproof. In addition, trying to walk and dig in a wet muddy field is hard messy work. If I am caught in a rain shower or storm, however, I have found that a waterproof cycling cape is best for maximum protection. Cycling shops should stock a range of them. The better type has a hood with a drawstring and a longer front designed to go out over the handlebars. This feature ensures that the detector is well covered from the rain. Those made from 100 per cent polyester can be folded up into a small pouch that is only the size of a drinks bottle. Many of the makes have a loop on the pouch so it can be carried easily on your equipment belt.

**Footwear.** The same advice applies as for outer clothing. Visit a reputable outdoor walking shop and get a pair of really comfortable boots with good ankle support. These are also frequently available with a Gore-Tex lining for added comfort. A ploughed field can be an easy place to break an ankle when wearing inappropriate footwear. Of course, if the ground is wet what you really need are good-quality Wellington boots.

If you go to an industrial clothing supplier for your footwear, you will be guaranteed plenty of good signals while out detecting – but probably not the ones you want. In order to meet health and safety regulations, work boots have to be made with steel toecaps. This warning also applies to other footwear: check for metal eyelets, lace ends or other metal trimmings.

**Ancillary Equipment**

The first item of equipment that you will require is something to help you carry and organize the many things we need with us. This could be a backpack, while some detectorists carry everything in the pockets of their clothing. Some of the variants of workers' tool belts that have recently come on the market look as though they could be useful to the detectorist. The best solution to the problem that I have found, however, is to use military pattern webbing. This has the advantage that it has been battle proven. Troops regularly carry as much as 10kg of equipment around their waist. From our point of view the benefits are in the stability and distribution of the load we will be carrying. The best place to locate a supply of ex-military or police SWAT kit is via the Internet, where plenty of army surplus suppliers are listed.

When deciding what to buy, make a list of all the pockets or pouches you need. By way of example, and in no particular order, you will need to accommodate some or all of the following:

- First aid kit
- Mobile phone
- GPS unit
- Spare batteries (charged)
- Marker flag
- Knife, whistle, torch
- Spares
- Magnifying glass

*There is a wide range of coil sizes available and dealers will make recommendations for your type of detecting.*

- Rain cape
- Finds pouch
- Junk pouch

Give the choice careful consideration; if you are not comfortable and settled while detecting you will miss those faint signals. One thing you need to take on board at an early stage is that a large part of detecting is about concentrating and interpreting the signals accurately.

## Coils

Your machine will come with a standard size coil that is normally between 20cm and 25cm in diameter. These are good general-purpose coils, but the more experienced detectorist will probably acquire some of the other size coils available. Smaller coils (10–15cm in diameter) are used to winkle out good signals on sites that have a large amount of junk. Small coils can also be particularly useful in woods or forests, enabling you to get the coil between saplings and roots. The larger coils, which are typically up to 70cm in diameter, are useful when you want to cover large areas such as fields or beaches, but you should be aware that they can add considerably to the weight and therefore the strain on your arm.

## Coil Covers

Coil covers are moulded plastic covers used to protect the underside of the coil from the cuts and scratches it receives as it is scuffed over the ground during the search sweep (or it should if you are detecting properly). They do not affect the performance of the detector in any way. They are essential to prevent expensive damage to the coil: a new coil can easily cost as much as £200.

*A coil cover (here one made by Minelab) is a wise investment that will save you money over the years.*

### Headphones

Buy the very best headphones that you can afford. Using high-quality headphones can enhance a low-cost detector's performance. On the other hand, detecting with a top quality detector but making do with budget-priced headphones will result in many signals of a faint or weak nature being missed.

The superior headphones best suited for the hobby are all based on good-quality ear defenders. This ensures that any external noise sources caused by wind or traffic, for example, will be blanked out. Make sure that the headphones you buy are constructed using solid-state components that ensure high-performance sound reproduction in field conditions. At the time of writing headphones of this standard are likely to cost in excess of £60.

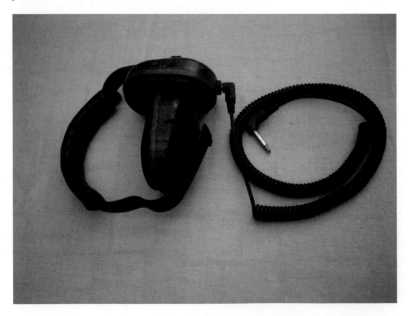

*With headphones you get what you pay for, so spend as much as you can afford on purpose-made examples.*

*A good-quality bag will protect your machine from knocks and bangs. This example is fitted with a thermal lining.*

### Carry Bag

It is prudent to use a protective soft, shower-proof bag to transport your detector. When you may have spent perhaps as much as £1,000 on your detector it is of utmost importance that it is protected from shocks and external damage. This will ensure optimum performance in the field. Dealers should be able to supply one to suit your machine.

Many Detectorists see ancillary equipment as an unimportant part of the hobby. However, if you are going to be successful you need the 'complete package'. A good detector on its own is not enough.

**Be prepared, be organized.
Failing to plan is planning to fail.**

# CHAPTER 8

# SEARCHING FOR SITES AND COMMUNITY OPPORTUNITIES

There are many ways to carry out research when looking for sites and land to detect on. Most of these can be grouped into one of four categories:

- the Internet
- maps
- books
- verbal information

## THE INTERNET

Research today has been made a lot easier with the introduction of the World Wide Web or Internet. Information that could have taken days or even weeks to unearth in the past can now be tracked down in minutes. The best starting point is often one of the numerous mapping sites: one of these even specializes in maps from the nineteenth century. The value of the Internet can be seen in the following example.

My wife recently found a particularly fine silver coin while detecting in France. It had quite distinctive markings and the date 1576 was clearly visible. We decided that it would make for some interesting research on our return home. On our way back to Calais, however, we visited Dave Ebbage at his house in Normandy. The silver coin caught his eye and within an hour he had not only sourced the identity of the coin but had even traced the mint where it had been struck.

The coin turned out to be a 1576 double sol parisis of Henri III (reg 1574–89). The mint mark revealed that it had been struck in Montpellier in southern France. This is only 35km from where the coin was found, on a major bridle path route near Béziers.

A list of useful websites covering many subjects may be found in Useful Contacts.

## MAPS

Old maps can be a valuable source of information, showing all manner of features that have long since disappeared, including hamlets, villages, racecourses and even fairgrounds. A map covering my local area recently helped me find the location of an old oak tree used for public hangings.

Aerial photographs have the great advantage that they can show a wealth of features not visible at ground level. The most easily accessible source of aerial photographs is via the Google Earth website. In order to start exploring this remarkable source, visit earth.google.co.uk/ and download the free software.

It is proposed that the national archive of military aerial reconnaissance photos taken during the Second World War will be made available to the public in 2010. This will undoubtedly indicate some very interesting sites for searching, such as the location of camps, grass airfields and aircraft crash sites, both in the United Kingdom and abroad. It will still be necessary, of course, to obtain the correct permissions before going on to anybody's land.

## BOOKS

The local and central libraries in your area are the prime starting point for research using books. All libraries in the United Kingdom have a computerized search facility for all published books. Even if the particular book you want is not available from stock, the librarian can request their County Office to purchase a copy of it if they consider there will be sufficient demand. My local library, for example, recently purchased a book that I had been trying to source with their help; it was not too expensive, at a little over £12, but this shows that the system works.

Newspapers can provide information on local and national subjects. Most have easily accessible archives and many of these have been made available on the Internet. Keep your eyes open for advertisements and reports on events such as fairs, parades, markets, car boot sales, and sites where the public could pick their own fruit. Look out for any references to old leisure activities that may no longer be in use, or old swimming areas in rivers and lakes. Watch out for street names that may give a clue to their previous use. The Butts, for example, was the area for archery practice in medieval times, while Fairfield in my own town is where all the fairs and sales have been held for many years and it is still used for this purpose.

*Watch out for clues as to what may have happened on the site in years gone by.*

Specialist books are also available from the metal-detecting dealers, detecting magazines and, of course, a metal-detecting club's own library.

Some years ago I wanted to identify some sites that might be worth detecting abroad. One area that appealed to me was northern Spain and Portugal, particularly those parts of the countryside that had been occupied by the armies of both sides during the Peninsular War in the early nineteenth century. It transpired that the novels written by Bernard Cornwell about the exploits of the infamous Richard Sharpe, under the command of the Duke of Wellington, were so accurate historically and geographically that they could be used to help identify possible sites. This shows that not all the books used in research have to be heavy reading.

## VERBAL INFORMATION

This area of research is not often exploited by detectorists as much as it should be. The best starting point is neighbours, work colleagues and friends. This is an operation known in business circles as networking. Ask if anyone knows of any land that you could detect on or if they can suggest someone who does. Never overlook an opportunity to enquire whether anyone has lost something, such as keys, jewellery or any metal objects, of actual or sentimental value.

Using this networking method I have acquired not only land to detect on but also many friends and well-wishers after recovering items they had lost. It is a good idea to have signs and cards made up announcing that you carry out a 'Free Finds Service'. This can give the detectorist some

---

### Free recovery service

Lost a ring or article of sentimental value?

For FREE recovery service, provided the loss was on open land and the approximate location is known,

contact: *(insert your contact details)*

The above mentioned is a member of the Federation of Independent Detectorists, carries and identity card and is covered by £5,000,000 Public Liability Insurance.

Members have located many thousands of lost items for councils, farmers, vets, public services, tourists and the general public.

---

### Service gratuity de recuperation

Avez vous perdu une bague ou un object de valeur sentimentale?

Si oui

Service gratuity offert sur terrain public (plag, mer) ou autorise

Le non ci-dessus est un member de la Federation Independante des Detecteurs

Et est porteur d'une cart d'identite.

*(insert your contact details)*

---

### Servicio de Recubrimiento Gratis

¿ Ha perdido anillo o articulo de valor sentimental?

Si la perdida fue en terreno abierto y si saba approximadamente adonde fue,

Pongase en contacto con *(insert your contact details)*

Membro de la Federacion de Detectoristas Independientes (Gran Bretaña)

---

*Suggested text for cards advertising a 'Free Finds Service', in English, French and Spanish.*

credibility with members of the public and when dealing with local authorities and the police, particularly if you carry a photo identity card.

The Federation of Independent Detectorists (FID) issues an excellent example of an ID card that also covers members with liability insurance of up to £5,000,000. This is an organization I would strongly recommend to individuals active in the hobby.

Joining your local historical society can be a good way of expanding your knowledge of the area and its history. In fact many local organizations are worth contacting as their members are often from the more mature part of the community and they therefore have memories from times before rules stopped many leisure activities taking place, such as information about swimming spots on rivers and lakes.

The Silver Threads and Age Concern club in the town in which I live have more than a hundred regular members. Since their average age is about 78, that provides some 7,800 years of memories I can access when researching local sites. My experience has shown that people from these age groups are very willing to reminisce about their past experiences.

## GOODWILL AND COMMUNITY RELATIONS

Both the hobby and the individual can win a wealth of goodwill by helping various groups within the community. Advertise your 'Free Finds Service' wherever you can. Parish magazines, the post office, newsagents and even your own front window or gate post are just a few of the places worth trying.

I have obtained permission to detect on several pieces of land after being asked to carry out searches by members of the public. This system has worked well in England and, with the notice

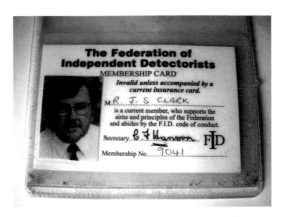

*Always carry a photo ID card with you. Such cards are mandatory in many European countries. (Federation of Independent Detectorists)*

translated into Spanish and French, has been most useful abroad.

While carrying out searches on holiday I have successfully recovered car keys, apartment keys, a gold earring, a wedding ring and several dress rings for members of the public. One unusual request was to find the credit card-type ignition key from a new Renault Laguna. There was a problem in that it appears to be made of plastic and I did not know what signal I would need to listen for, but a visit to the local Renault dealer revealed that the magnetic strip within the card provided a quite distinctive double beep signal with a tone similar to silver. I eventually found the key in calf-length grass, standing vertically between the tall grass blades. It is extremely unlikely that it would ever have been found without the use of a metal detector.

Cultivate a good relationship with local authorities and councils. After an article appeared in our local evening newspaper concerning razor blades found among the bark chippings under the swings in the children's play area, I contacted the Clerk of Council and offered to detect the park using my metal detector and recover all metal objects. After discussing the matter the council accepted and I later received written authority to detect on *all* council land. Since the town can trace its roots back to Saxon times, who knows what may turn up in the future. What was interesting was the range of finds recovered from just one play area: nuts and bolts, screws, broken bottles (some still with their metal tops), pieces of wire, even a used hypodermic syringe. The last of these shows that you must be careful. Before you touch anything like this, make sure you get the correct training and handling equipment from the council. The search also turned up some coins, which went into the council office's tea fund.

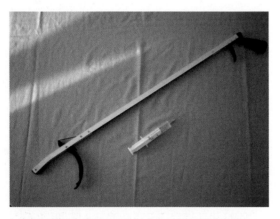

*If you find a hypodermic syringe, it should only be handled with a remote picker. Local councils may well provide training and offer to loan you the correct equipment to deal with such items.*

Make the local police aware of your ability to search for and recover lost or discarded items. When people report the loss of small metal items, the police will often give them the details of a local detectorist who offers a 'Free Finds Service'. Occasionally detectorists have been asked to assist the police in the hunt for items that may be part of a crime, particularly if the search is within woodland or roadside ditches and fields. It is not only weapons that are metal; many items of clothing and footwear have metal components within them.

You can help to raise awareness of metal detecting by giving talks to groups and clubs within the local community. This can also be a productive way of meeting individuals willing to give permission to search their land. When concluding a talk I usually offer to show individuals or a small group of two or three how detectors work in the field, using one of my spare detectors. Invariably the offer is taken up and, living in a semi-rural area, it is not unusual to find a landowner within the group. After the demonstration there is often an invitation to return and detect on their land.

> **Researching sites is like being a detective. You must use your little grey cells.**

# CHAPTER 9

# FINDING LAND TO DETECT ON

Having taken the effort to carry out your research, buy a detector and learn how to use it, it is not much good unless you are able to acquire some land upon which you can carry out your hobby.

Perhaps the most obvious place you should start on is your own land, which for most people will be their garden, or perhaps gardens belonging to other members of their family. Some tremendous finds have come from gardens over the years.

A man who lived in a village in North Wiltshire had been detecting for quite a few years, mainly on land where permission had been acquired by the metal detecting club he belonged to. He had only limited success during this time, with no 'star quality' finds. As he was having an extension built onto his house, he took the opportunity to examine the spoil dug out for the new foundations. Every scoop of earth the digger excavated was placed on the ground in such a way that he was able to search it thoroughly before it was covered by a further scoopful. In this way several Victorian coins, old military buttons and some old iron tools were found.

Several days of rain brought work on the extension to a halt. Before the builders returned he had another go at the piles of spoil, which by now had been reduced in height and spread out by the heavy rain. Bearing in mind that most detectors only pick up signals in the top 30cm of the ground being searched, he estimated that the piles of earth had been reduced in height by some 40cm, so he was in effect detecting a completely fresh site. There were no fresh finds of any significance until his detector received an extremely strong signal that he was convinced indicated a large piece of metal, perhaps aluminium. Notwithstanding this, he decided to dig the signal, if only to eliminate it.

After careful digging he was amazed to see what turned out to be two arms of an ornately decorated cross protruding out of the earth. He continued to dig and eventually recovered a heavy silver cross, 23cm high and weighing nearly 500 grams.

He followed the correct procedures and reported his find to the Coroner as possibly Treasure. Eventually the cross was returned to him, to keep or dispose of as he wished. Later that year he decided to send the cross for auction in London, where it raised nearly £10,000. The moral is to exhaust the possibilities on your own, your family's and your friends' land before taking the more difficult route of obtaining permission from strangers.

## COLD CALL LETTER SAMPLE

Your name

Address

Telephone number

E-mail address

Date

Dear Mr/Mrs XXXXXX

Allow me to introduce myself. My name is XXXXX XXXXXXX and I have lived in 'Little Town' for XX years with my wife and two children. We take an active part in the local community. I felt that an initial contact by letter would break the ice.

I would like to offer my metal detecting services to you and any of your friends. There is no charge for my services as the thrill of the hunt more than compensates me.

I am an active exponent of the hobby and am a member of the **XXXX XXXXXX XXXX** Detecting Club. It is an absorbing and interesting hobby, which at times can be exciting and rewarding.

I have helped the **XXXX** Town Council by carrying out free safety sweeps of the children's playgrounds and sports fields. The public locally have benefited from the free recovery service I provide for items that have been lost.

Please understand that I pride myself in leaving the search area as I find it and any metal rubbish I may find is removed for responsible recycling.

After 7 to 10 days I will phone to make an appointment to meet you, at a time to suit you and your work schedule. I look forward to explaining my hobby to you in more detail.

Thank you for your time

Yours sincerely,

*Your signature here*

Your name printed

*Permission to detect on this land in the Spanish Pyrenees was obtained simply by asking the farmer who was working there.*

Not all of us are blessed with natural sales skills; this can make cold calling on farmers and landowners a pretty daunting prospect for many people. Some basic ground rules can improve the prospect of obtaining land to detect on.

## CONTACTING LANDOWNERS

It is good practice to carry out some simple research concerning the landowner you intend to approach prior to your first contact: the day they are about to start their main harvest, or one when foot-and-mouth disease is discovered in the area, is not going to be the best time to talk to them about detecting.

Make an effort to meet the people who work at the local agricultural merchants and gently probe as to which of the farmers and landowners among their customers are the most approachable. Tell them why you wish to contact them and also leave a card offering your 'Free Finds Service'. Many farmers may have lost tools, small parts from machines or even personal items while out working out on their land, and they may be grateful if you are able to recover these items for them. Even if you cannot find the lost item on your first attempt, offer to come back for another go and ask if you can detect anywhere else on their land. It is unusual for them to turn down the offer after you have spent several hours looking for their lost property.

Another method of finding land is via a 'cold call' letter, followed seven or ten days later with a phone call. Names and addresses of farmers

## SAMPLE CONTRACT

### SEARCH AGREEMENT

Date _____ Landowner/owner _____

Address _____

_____

Telephone _____ E-mail _____

Description of the area for detecting [attach a plan or map] _____

_____

Detectorist _____

Address _____

_____

Telephone _____ E-mail _____

1. Permission is granted to detect using a metal detector and hand tools to locate and recover items found on the above-mentioned land.

2. This agreement shall run until either side cancels it in writing and cannot be assigned to a third party.

3. Livestock and wildlife, be it animal or plant, must be respected and protected at all times.

4. The Detectorist will immediately inform the Landowner of any finds that are of more than £10 in value or are covered by the Treasure Act.

5. The Detectorist will inform the Coroner of any finds covered by the Treasure Act within 14 days of realizing that the item is in fact Treasure.

6. The Detectorist will report any archaeological finds to the Landowner and is responsible for reporting finds to the Finds Liaison Officer at the local museum.

7. The Detectorist will mark and report any bombs, munitions or dangerous finds to the police.

8. Both the Detectorist and the Landowner will own any finds that are covered by the Treasure Act, or are valued at £100 or more, on a 50–50 basis.

9. Any expenses incurred in valuing and disposing of any items covered by item 8 will be shared on a 50–50 split between the Detectorist and the Landowner.

Signed _____ Signed _____

Landowner _____ Detectorist _____

Date _____ Date _____

in your area may be found in local trade directories. The accompanying example of a letter I have used should provide some guidance as to what to say.

## ALTERNATIVE WAYS OF OBTAINING PERMISSION

In case you are the kind of person who finds the prospect of cold calling too daunting to contemplate, there are a number of options open to you:

- Team up with a detecting partner who has the natural ability to cold call and sell the idea of metal detecting to farmers and landowners.
- Plenty of metal-detecting rallies are advertised in *The Searcher* and *Treasure Hunting*. If you are a member of the Federation of Independent Detectorists, its quarterly newsletter has information and contact details of forthcoming rallies. Some of these are organized to raise funds for charities, such as a detecting rally promoted every year in North Wiltshire by the local Rotary Club.
- Join a detecting club that has a portfolio of land upon which regular searches are organized. These typically take place at the weekend every other week.
- Many of the detecting retailers put on rallies during the summer months to promote their business. Details may be found in the specialist press.
- Try beach detecting on public beaches. Permission is not normally required, but

do check with the beach rangers if the beach is manned. The best time is either early morning or evening time during the summer, or alternatively any time during the low season. (For more on this subject see Chapter 12.)

## CONTRACTUAL ARRANGEMENTS

Obtaining permission is only the beginning of the relationship with the landowner. They have every right to want the Ts crossed and the Is dotted before they allow you onto their land. I have a very simple contract with my landowners: anything I find is divided equally between us. Any expenses incurred after the find (during its appraisal, valuation and possible sale) will also be split fifty-fifty. This is all laid out plainly in the accompanying example of a simple contract. In addition there are many variations available, some of which have been professionally produced by clubs and organizations within the hobby.

It is important to maintain friendly personal relations with landowners. At the end of each year I make a point of creating a display of some of the artefacts I have found on the land. I then give this to the landowner at Christmas, together with a bottle of 'good cheer', thus ensuring another year's amicable detecting.

A really good place to detect is where you find something good!

# CHAPTER 10

# METAL DETECTING AND THE LAW

Many years ago I saw this anonymous statement, which has a certain irony for the detectorist.

Most countries have treasure trove laws. These are simple. All belongs to the state, which may reward you or punish you, depending on who your friends are.

A reading of the 1996 Treasure Act, however, lays things out in fairly straightforward terms.

## SUMMARY OF THE TREASURE ACT

The following finds are Treasure under the Act, if found after 24 September 1997 (or, in the case of category 2, if found after 1 January 2003):

1. Any metallic object, other than a coin, provided that at least 10 per cent by weight of metal is precious metal (that is, gold or silver) and that it is at least 300 years old when found. If the object is of prehistoric date it will be Treasure provided any part of it is precious metal.
2. Any group of two or more metallic objects of any composition of prehistoric date that come from the same find (see below).

3. All coins from the same find provided they are at least 300 years old when found (but if the coins contain less than 10 per cent of gold or silver there must be at least ten of them). Only the following groups of coins will normally be regarded as coming from the same find:

   - hoards that have been deliberately hidden
   - smaller groups of coins, such as the contents of purses, that may have been dropped or lost
   - ritual deposits.

4. Any object, whatever it is made of, that is found in the same place as, or had previously been together with, another object that is Treasure.
5. Any object that would previously have been treasure trove, but does not fall within the specific categories given above. Only objects that are less than 300 years old, that are made substantially of gold or silver, that have been deliberately hidden with the intention of recovery and whose owners or heirs are unknown will come into this category.

**Note:**

An object or coin is part of the 'same find' as another object or coin if it is found in the same place as, or had previously been together with, the other object. Finds may have become scattered since they were originally deposited in the ground.

*Reporting Finds*

You must report all finds of Treasure to a coroner for the district in which they are found, either within fourteen days after the day on which you made the discovery or within fourteen days after the day on which you realized the find might be treasure. Details of your local coroner may be found in a telephone directory or online.

### Portable Antiquities Scheme

At the same time that the new Treasure Act came into force (March 1996), the Portable Antiquities Scheme was created to record all small finds or portable antiquities under direction of the Department of Portable Antiquities and Treasure at the British Museum. Access to the scheme is via the Finds Liaison Officer for your area, who is usually located in the County Museum.

*A range of information is available on all aspects of the rules and laws relevant to metal detecting.*

## THE NATIONAL COUNCIL FOR METAL DETECTING CODE OF CONDUCT

1. Do not trespass. Obtain permission before venturing onto any land.
2. Respect the Country Code. Do not leave gates open and do not damage crops or frighten animals.
3. Wherever the site, do not leave a mess or an unsafe surface for those who may follow. It is perfectly simple to extract a coin or other small object buried a few inches below the ground without digging a great hole. Use a suitable digging implement to cut a neat flap (do not remove the plug of earth entirely from the ground). Extract the object, reinstate the grass, sand or soil carefully and even you will have difficulty in locating the find spot again.
4. If you discover any live ammunition or any lethal object, such as an unexploded bomb or mine, do not disturb it. Mark the site carefully and report the find to the local police and landowner.
5. Help keep Britain tidy. Safely dispose of refuse you come across.
6. Report all unusual historical finds to the landowner and acquaint yourself with current NCMD policy relating to the Voluntary Reporting of Portable Antiquities.
7. Remember it is illegal for anyone to use a metal detector on a protected area (e.g. scheduled archaeological site, SSSI, or Ministry of Defence property) without permission from the appropriate authority.
8. Acquaint yourself with the definitions of Treasure contained in the Treasure Act 1996 and its associated Code of Practice, making sure you understand your responsibilities.
9. Remember that when you are out with your metal detector you are an ambassador for our hobby. Do nothing that might give it a bad name.
10. Never miss an opportunity to explain your hobby to anyone who asks about it.

The Portable Antiquities Scheme is a voluntary scheme to record archeological items found by members of the public in England and Wales. Every year many thousands of objects are discovered, many by metal-detector users, but also by people walking, gardening or going about their daily work. At the time of writing some 200,000 items found by detectorists had been recorded via the scheme. Such discoveries offer an important source for understanding our past.

The British Museum website is a valuable source of information on all aspects of the Treasure Act and The Portable Antiquities Scheme (see www.britishmuseum.org/the_museum/departments/portable_antiquities_treasure.aspx). It is all explained in plain English with many onward references.

## CIVIL, CRIMINAL AND COMMON SENSE LAW

Law in this sense is not only that which is enforced by the courts, but also the due consideration for others that we should all obey.

### Civil Law

I cannot imagine that any detectorist would willingly become involved with any aspect of civil law. Questions of ownership concerning finds are best settled amiably as the financial costs of going to a civil court are prohibitive. Always be very careful if you find yourself coming up against local authorities. They can spend a lot of money on their rights, since it's not their money. It is far better to turn away and live to fight another day.

**(English)**

If you have lost a metal item on the beach in the last few days please ask, as it is possible I may have found it, or can try to find it.

**(Spanish)**

Si usted ha perdido algún artículo en la playa recientemente, por favor aviseme. Pues es posible que lo haya encontrado. Puedo intentar encontrarlo, si usted quiere.

**(French)**

Avez-vous perdu quelque chose de métallique sur la plage, récemment? Il est possible que je l'aie trouvé, ou je peux vous aider, le chercher. Demandez-moi, s'il vous plaît.

*This text is displayed in our motorhome windscreen, as part of taking 'reasonable steps' to find the owner.*

## Criminal Law

It is easy to fall foul of the criminal law if you act with ignorance or stupidity. The act of going onto someone's land without permission and carrying a detector is seen in law as 'going equipped to steal'. Heavy penalties can be imposed, so *don't do it*.

A further offence is that of 'stealing by finding'. If you find any modern items you must take reasonable steps to find the owner. If you find a gold ring, for example, hand it in to the police; if the item is not claimed within a period of time (typically three months), it will then be returned to you. Under British law you do not become the owner, but you do have 'title' to the item, which is nearly the same. Isn't the law clear?

Another 'reasonable step' you could take to comply with the law is to advertise your finds (for examples of the sign I use in English, French and Spanish, see left). The local Policia Civil in Spain has always been complimentary about the results and I have been able to return many items, including apartment keys, car keys, prescription glasses and jewellery. Perhaps the strangest object I have been asked to search for is the set of false teeth that a Spanish man lost in the surf. After searching for several hours I still didn't find them, but it does make a good after-dinner story.

## Common Sense Law

This covers any codes of practice that involve consideration for others. Always follow the advice given in the Countryside Code and the Coast Watch Code. Recommendations for best practice within the hobby are also available from the Federation of Independent Detectorists (FID) and the National Council for Metal Detecting (NCMD).

Be considerate when detecting, observe all codes and stay within the law.

# CHAPTER 11

# INLAND DETECTING

Land detecting in many areas is restricted due to the type of crops grown by the farmers. If you live in an arable farming area you will have to consult closely with landowners to find out what time of year you will and will not be allowed onto the land. They are certainly not going to want you tramping over the fields when the peas, beans, corn or barley are maturing. We all need to be aware that these crops represent a huge cash investment by the farmer, who has more than enough problems to live with during the life cycle of the crop, including disease, wind, drought and floods.

An agricultural policy that has helped the detectorist has been the designation of 'set-aside' land that the farmer is paid not to farm; he is not even allowed to plough it. The European Union has recently proposed that the amount of set-aside land permitted on each farm will be reduced from 10 per cent down to 5 per cent. There will be fewer problems with access to pasture land if you live in an area where livestock farming is the norm. Unlike ploughed fields, pasture can be accessed most of the year. The only restrictions on the farm will be when the young animals are being born.

The discovery of any disease such as foot-and-mouth, bird flu or swine fever, however, can have a drastic effect on detecting opportunities on cattle and animal farms. If any of these diseases is declared in your area you must observe all the restrictions that are imposed. Do not be tempted to break these rules under any circumstances. Head for the beach and leave inland detecting alone for a while. Have sympathy for the farmers, as they may be going through a very difficult and stressful time. But you may find that you could earn yourself some brownie points for when things return to normal by offering to help around the farm, doing some disinfecting and clearing up.

Wherever you use your detector inland, the methods adopted will vary according to which of the two categories of search you are observing: opportunity detecting or targeted detecting.

## OPPORTUNITY DETECTING

The first is opportunity detecting, in which the opportunity to detect on some land may arise purely by chance. This might come after a talk you have given or from a response to a newspaper article on your involvement in the hobby. It can also occur as a result of somebody seeing you detecting and inviting you to try your hand on their land or when your cold calling or telephone canvassing pays dividends.

Beggars cannot be choosers. Even if the land on offer does not appear to be too promising, give it a go. Before you start, try to do some research concerning the history of the land; you may find that it has been occupied for several

*There are occasions when farmers may be happy for you to use your equipment on their land. Here the field has been ploughed and harrowed, but has not yet been seeded. The harrow marks in the soil make it easy to set up a gridiron search pattern.*

thousand years and not just for the last few. Try to discover what the land has been used for and if there are any signs of old buildings. Examine the images of the area on Google Earth to see if there are any shadows on the landscape that might indicate previous occupation of the site, even going as far back as earthworks from pre-historic and proto-historic periods.

When travelling about your area keep your eyes open for signs of where farmers are clearing their hedges and dredging the ditches. This kind of work provides the detectorist with an opportunity to detect the spoil from the sites and some very significant finds have come from freshly excavated earth.

In and around Wiltshire it is not unusual to find that farmland was used during both World Wars for the temporary billeting of troops In tented camps. Always ask the landowners and perhaps their older relatives if they have any knowledge of what used to go on in the area. It may turn out that horse or goose fairs were held on the land, or perhaps there were swimming sites along a river that crosses their land.

If you belong to a detecting club that has obtained permission to detect over a particular stretch of land, do not think that it will be cleaned out of finds just because the club has been going there for several years. As I have said before, most of the time we were only sampling the ground and significant finds have come from club sites that have been visited time and time again. So be optimistic and take heart from the discovery of a Roman hoard described in Chapter 16.

## TARGETED DETECTING

The second type of inland detecting is on targeted land. This where detectorists have carried out their research into an event or site and eventually narrowed down their search to the actual piece of land they wish to detect on, which may be as small as a single dwelling. Perhaps the easiest way to show how this type of targeted detecting can be used is to look at some examples.

A few years ago a group of detectors in Wiltshire wanted to find the remains of a German Heinkel 111 twin-engine bomber that was reputed to have been shot down on the Wiltshire border, close to the town of Hungerford, during the night of 29/30 June 1940 following an air raid on the Great Western Railway Works in Swindon. (For further background information, see www.ramsburyatwar.com.)

The only planes in the area were reported to have climbed to the west after dropping their bombs, before taking the usual route of following the railway lines to Chippenham (the polished lines glint, even in the dark) and then turning south to the Dorset coast and on to their bases in Northern France. The records of aircraft sightings for that night, however, suggested that, although six planes had taken part in the raid on Swindon, only four enemy aircraft were reported as passing east of Chippenham following a southerly route. So two planes would appear to be 'missing'.

More than a year later they had a breakthrough while detecting in the village of Lambourne, east of Swindon. There appeared to be a large number of spent bullets. Most were undamaged but some were deformed, showing they had hit something in anger. In conversation with an octogenarian farmer, it appeared that the undamaged bullets would have come from fighter pilots testing their machine guns after taking off from Membury airfield nearby. The damaged bullets, however, all came from a particular area where

*A small selection of spent munitions.*

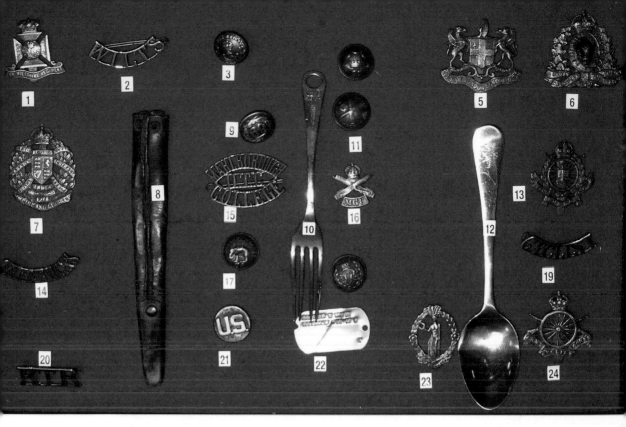

An excellent display of military badges, many from the vicinity of Chiseldon Camp, Wiltshire, that represents hours of research, cleaning and setting out. (Collection and display by Kenneth James; photo by Brian Cavill)

1 Wilts Regiment cap badge, 1914
2 Wilts shoulder title, curved version 1902 on
3 Button, Rifle Brigade, World War II
4 Button, 23rd Regiment of Foot (Royal Welsh Fusiliers) 1855–c.1860
5 Cap badge, City of London School, OT Corps
6 Cap badge, Royal Canadian Mounted Police
7 Cap badge, 2nd King Edwards Horse, 1914
8 Stiletto or dagger sheath, believed American, World War II
9 69 Regiment of Foot, South Lincolnshire
10 NAAFI issue dining fork
11 Button, Machine Gun Corps, World War I
12 US issue dining spoon (Medical Corps)
13 Cap badge, City of London 1st Division Cycle Company (formed in 1916 and disbanded after three months)
14 Shoulder title Ox & Bucks, curved version work with separate bugle until 1954
15 Shoulder tab, World War I, Marlborough OTC College
16 Collar badge, Machine Gun Corps, World War I
17 Button, 76th Regiment of Foot, 1855–81
18 Button, general issue, Victorian period
19 Shoulder title, Army Cyclist Corps, World War I
20 Shoulder title, Royal Tank Regiment, 1939
21 Button, US Army, World War II
22 US serviceman's identity tag, World War II
23 Cap badge, Women's Legion 1915 (cooks, drivers, etc.; formed by Lady Londonderry)
24 Cap badge, Army Cyclist Corps, 1914

one of two large aircraft, flying in the wrong direction and sounding 'different', was shot down by anti-aircraft guns and fighters scrambled to protect the airfield. The wreckage was now buried deep in the hill, where the hole was filled in quickly so farming could continue.

They had definitely found a plane, but was it the one they were looking for? Were these the two Heinkels that went missing between Swindon and Chippenham? Had they merely become disorientated after the raid and headed east instead of west? There remains a great deal of research to be done, but at least they now have a lead.

Targeted detecting requires extreme patience. You must be prepared to waste time down blind alleys before you finally reach your goal. It can easily take several years, but it feels good when all that detective work pays off and you reach a successful conclusion.

A fellow club member specializes in detecting for military artefacts. His approach is to research a site from the local historical records, mainly found via the library and on the Internet, and then to find out from Land Registry who has title to the land. He follows this by creating a folder showing the history of the site with photos, text and sometimes film or video footage. He then approaches the landowners and gives them a presentation of his findings. This is often the first time that they are aware of the historical events that have taken place on their land.

Many sites in North Wiltshire and West Berkshire have been occupied by the Army and RAF. Some were occupied for as little as four months prior to the D-Day landings in June 1944. From a detectorist's point of view these sites are a rich source of artefacts, illustrated on page 91, that provide an insight into a unique period in our nation's history.

# INLAND DETECTING IN EUROPE

The same principles can be applied to finding land to detect on if you are interested in detecting abroad. It is of course more difficult to secure the necessary permission unless you can speak the language. I am fortunate in that I can speak French, German and Spanish well enough for my needs. If you do not speak the language, however, one way around the problem is to make contact with your local Twinning Association, who may be able to put you in touch with someone in the town with which they are twinned. You may even be lucky enough to find another detectorist. Those who join twinning associations do so to meet people from their twinned town and, in my experience, many of them speak English.

Before moving to a village near Mayenne in Normandy, Dave Ebbage was a very experienced detectorist and Site Officer of my club in North Wiltshire. His personal account opposite of the very different world of detecting in France provides a valuable guide to what you may expect across the English Channel.

> Opportunities always look best going away. Learn to recognize them when they are in front of you.

## METAL DETECTING IN FRANCE *by Dave Ebbage*

Whereas in the United Kingdom there may be as many as 30,000 detectorists and more than seventy clubs, in France the hobby is not as popular and is conducted on a more individual basis with only the largest towns having clubs. According to the website of the Fédération Nationale des Utilisateurs de Détecteurs de Métaux (FNUDM, www.prospection. net), there are about thirty-three *associations* (clubs) in France. Rallies are rare with perhaps two or three each year. These events are large, but considerable travel is needed and a two hour lunch is essential to enjoy the full benefit of the rally! In the five years

I have been living in France I have yet to see anyone detecting in the countryside.

I have been fortunate in obtaining permission from many farmers to detect on their lands – the first farmer I asked wanted to know how much I would charge him. The population density of the country is about half that of the United Kingdom. In the past people lived isolated existences in small towns and villages, rarely travelling more than a few kilometres from their birthplace. Even after a true national coinage was introduced, trade was often carried out using bartering. The Napoleonic inheritance laws, which

*French magazines on metal detecting are rarely on sale in shops and are best obtained by post. (David Ebbage)*

## METAL DETECTING IN FRANCE *(continued)*

made it mandatory for children to take priority over all other family members, including spouses, tended to reinforce this pattern and there is still a strong resistance to leaving one's home town or village.

Many invaders have passed across the landscape – Goths, Visigoths, Romans, English, Spanish and Germans, to name but a few – and one would expect to find an interesting mix of coins and artefacts. But this has not been the case in my experience. I live in Département 53, the Mayenne and a part of the Pays de la Loire, where farming is a major industry and there are many hectares of land available for searching around the village. There seems to be little involvement by archaeologists or indeed interest in the curtailment of detecting, although further north there may be restrictions in searching due to the numerous military sites and the possibility of uncovering wartime explosives. While it is difficult to give an objective comparison of

*Unusual French bicycle road tax discs. (David Ebbage)*

the find rate in France compared with Wiltshire, in terms of the quantity of non-ferrous items located my figures in France might be less than one-tenth of my UK finds. The number of coins, in particular, especially those minted before the Revolution, is low and to date I have not found a single silver coin. My oldest find in France has been the broken blade of a late Bronze Age axe, but most finds relate to the period after the Revolution. The most common coins come from the period of Napoleon III (reg 1852–70), the 50 centimes piece being the size of the old British halfpenny. Some unusual finds, unique to France, are the pre-war bicycle road tax tags.

French law regarding metal detecting is less formal than in the United Kingdom, although such is the legal system in France that a Napoleonic law can be found to deal with any situation! These are my own views, but in general there appear to be no problems with detecting on land without archaeological or historic backgrounds provided permission has been obtained from the landowner. To be more pedantic, because of the way land is frequently subdivided and often rented out, it may be difficult to locate the true owner of the land. All the farmers I have dealt with, however, have been helpful as well as very interested in our hobby. With regard to finds, the situation is similar for those classified as covered by the Treasure Act in the UK. In practice, it might only be necessary to record hoards with the local authorities. My own feelings are that smaller finds would be retained by the local administrations and never seen again – not due to theft, but to the incredible amount of bureaucracy found in France. My philosophy is to be honest and open-handed. Show all the finds to the landowner and, if necessary, the Mayor. So far this has proved most rewarding. I have had some contact with local archaeologists, mainly with regard to identifying finds, and they have been very helpful. In this respect I have also been involved in the renovation of a local château and was allowed by the Project Manager, who is not an archaeologist, to search the spoil heap and found a small coin weight. In the future I hope to extend my work on local archaeological digs.

Supporting the metal detectorists in France are dealers who offer a wide range of detecting products,

*French 2 franc coin (left) with the postwar (1945) declaration of Liberty, Equality and Fraternity, compared (right) with the exhortation under German occupation (1943) of Work, Family and Fatherland. (David Ebbage)*

including many also on sale in Britain. The French made XP range is available widely and seems to be extending its customer base to the UK (www.xpmetaldetectors.com). A Spanish detector that is available is known as the Deepers MF owing to its relatively low frequency of operation (it can be adjusted to 400 different frequencies ranging from 550Hz to 950 Hz; see www.deepers.com).

Detecting in France has not reached the level of interest or activity that it has attained in the United Kingdom, but there is potential for strong growth that could be well supported. Should you wish to detect in France, comply with my comments regarding obtaining permission and avoid archaeological or historic sites. The French equivalent of Google Earth, known as Géoportail (www.geoportail.fr), should help your research. You will find that the coverage of France is at a much higher resolution than Google Earth can offer, so giving you a head start in your detecting.

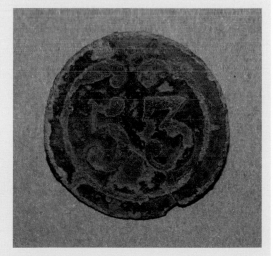

*French postman's button for Département 53 (Mayenne). (David Ebbage)*

# CHAPTER 12

# BEACH DETECTING

One important aspect of beach detecting is to ensure you have a machine capable of working on heavily mineralized ground and saltwater sand. Your detector dealer will advise you on this feature. Most beach machines can be used inland, but many machines designed for inland use may be unsuitable for the beach.

A type of machine favoured for use below the high-water mark is the pulse induction (PI) detector, which thrives in heavily mineralized and wet salt-sand conditions. It is not unusual for beaches to have a magnetized under-bed of black dense sand. This is good for holding coins and jewellery, but can cause problems for detectors incapable of ground balancing against the magnetic background.

When used above the high-water mark, the problem with PI machines is that they cannot discriminate out the large volume of junk, but further down the beach this becomes much less serious as the quantity of junk reduces dramatically. The junk you want to avoid consists of silver paper, ring-pulls and any ferrous items, such as bottle tops, dropped as litter on the beach.

*Sand that has been frothed up by the beach machine every day becomes very fine and powdery.*

For the drier area of the beach above the high-water mark, your best choice is a tone discriminating motion detector, which can discriminate out the junk. It is not unusual to use different types of detectors to get the best performance when operating on difficult mineralized ground.

The recovery of items from the beach can require a rather different approach from that used inland. Recovery from wet sand uses methods very similar to those described above (see page 49). When detecting on dry powdery sand, however, you will find that actually getting hold of the target with your fingers becomes more difficult owing to sand acting more like a fluid. This situation becomes only more frustrating as the sand gets dryer and of the finest type, until getting hold of the item is nearly impossible. To overcome this it is essential to buy a sand scoop. Beach recovery tools can make life so much easier. Locate the item and pinpoint it as usual, then recover the target with the scoop, shake out the sand and perhaps you may find treasure at the bottom of the scoop.

## THE EFFECT OF TIDES ON THE BEACH

The first thing we must do is to define what constitutes a 'beach' through looking at the tidal patterns occurring in the area we wish to search. The Bristol Channel, for example, has the second largest tidal rise and fall in the world. This means that the beaches can range in width from zero to more than a kilometre, depending on the state of the tide.

Always make sure, before you leave home, that your visit to a beach will coincide with a suitable period of low tide. In every period of twenty-four hours there are four tides, the pattern

*When the sand is soft always use a sand scoop.*

being 'high-low-high-low'. These are separated by approximately six hours, but it is most important to acquire a set of tide tables showing the tidal flow, not only in time but also in the form of a graph. While the high and low are roughly six hours apart, the rate of the flood (incoming) and the ebb (outgoing) is not linear and depends on the phase of the moon. The tide may ebb quickly and flood slowly, but at another time in the moon's cycle it can ebb slowly and flood quickly (for more on this subject, see Chapter 13). You can put yourself or your group in extreme danger if you are not aware of the tidal flow.

The most notorious example of this danger involved the death of twenty-three Chinese cockle pickers in Morecambe Bay during February 2004. The tidal phase that night was such that the water had gone out quickly and was held in a prolonged low tide. As the tide turned, the water came in a little to a depth of approximately 30cm and then held again. This depth was enough to turn the top surface of the sand into quicksand. Trapped in the sands, the cockle pickers were then at the mercy of the flood tide, which came in extremely quickly with disastrous consequences.

97

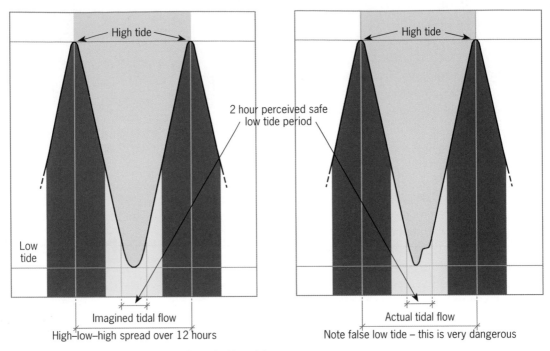

Graph demonstrating the course of a lethal low tide.

Anyone who tells you the best time to detect is two hours before low tide, for example, and two hours after is clearly oversimplifying things.

At the other extreme, we have the beaches around the Mediterranean. Although many people believe there is no tidal movement in the Mediterranean Sea, in fact there is a tide, but the difference between high and low tide is only about half a metre and so it has almost no effect on the area of dry beach available to search.

## KNOW YOUR BEACHES

Since most detectors will only search reliably to a depth of 30 to 40cm, you will need to build up a detailed knowledge of your search area and become familiar with it. Take photos of it every time you visit, in all types of light and weather conditions. Then keep them for comparison. Make notes on where there are any water gullies

after a storm (some of our best finds have come from deep gullies).

What happens within the area washed by the storm water? All the coins, jewellery and other objects dropped on that section of beach will have worked their way down into the sand and be at varying depths. Some on the base of the beach could even be up to 3m down, where they will have been since the beach was rebuilt by machines or nature following a previous storm.

Due to the differing specific gravity of the various items in the gully area – gold, for example, has an SG of 19.2 whereas sand has a specific gravity of between 2 and 3, depending on its geological make-up – we have a situation in which, once the storm water has passed through and washed away the sand, the lightest or lowest specific gravity material within the path of the water, all of the heavier items such as

ABOVE: *The beach at Jávea, Spain, before a storm; note the foot washes.*

BELOW: *24 hours later the foot washes at Jávea have been washed away by a flash storm overnight.*

*This storm gully, 1.8m deep, appeared overnight. Council tractors will be out repairing the beach within hours, so you need to work quickly to recover the finds.*

*It took only fourteen hours for this sand to be piled up against seafront apartments during a storm.*

coins and jewellery will now be within detector range in the floor of the gully. This makes it very easy to collect them. One gully that appeared overnight on a Spanish beach after a storm was 1.8m deep and within it were found more than seven pieces of jewellery and twenty-four coins. The area had been thoroughly detected two days previously, so the storm water did us a big favour by clearing away many tons of sand.

The effect the tides and currents have on where finds will be located is very important to the detectorist. Every beach or bay will be affected differently, so it is very important to get to know each area and keep a diary or make a log of its features and where the finds were located.

For more than ten years I have been making maps of bays that I visit, recording the differing patterns for spring and autumn, and the effect of winter storms. These maps have proved so useful that I can find money and jewellery time after time in the same detailed locations, sometimes

Finds area

*This natural sand and gravel spit on the Atlantic coast of Portugal provided some tremendous finds.*

from visits only four weeks apart. Sometimes the area will be as small as 10 by 20m. This shows that the tides and currents are sorting and depositing lost items of a similar density (or size and weight) in the same areas.

Another thing that is also happening to the seabed, depending on whether the winds are offshore or onshore, is that the sandbanks are shifting in, out and around the bay. This has the effect in some areas of covering items in deep sand or elsewhere of uncovering them as the sand is stripped away.

When studying any beach, always establish in which direction the waves travel. Are they travelling from left to right along the beach or from right to left? Around Britain the currents

*A man-made groyne viewed at low tide: the darker gravel shows where the inwash meets the outwash.*

Finds areas

Gravel & shell bed

*Obstructions along the beach cause the wave action to drop the finds regularly in certain places that you can return to time after time. The gravel and shell bed shown here is a classic example of what you should look out for.*

predominantly travel in a clockwise direction. Where the waves are travelling along the beach, even slightly, look for an obstruction of any kind – perhaps a groyne, a pier, jetty, breakwater or just a natural sand and gravel spit. The accompanying photographs indicate the best areas to search.

It is necessary to plot the movement of the waves during the whole cycle of the tide. What tends to happen is that the inwash (incoming wave) runs along the beach until it meets the obstruction. As the wave runs up and along it, coming inland, it will lose momentum before turning and becoming the outwash (outgoing wave). Where the outwash meets the inwash is exactly where coins, jewellery and artefacts moved about by the currents will be dropped. When this area is observed at low tide, the area to be searched will be indicated by the concentrated deposits of gravel, shells and other debris, some of which may be quite large. Get used

to recognizing the signs whenever you visit a beach.

Perhaps, as in some bays in the Mediterranean, the waves are coming straight in and up the beach. Under these conditions, there are three areas we must examine. The first is at the central peak of where the waves break upon the beach. The second and third places are where the outwash meets the inwash wave and creates an undertow. This may be indicated by waves breaking over submerged sandbanks. These points are normally either side of the centre point where the incoming waves break. It may take a few visits to a bay to establish the points to search. but once you have mapped them you can keep on returning to 'harvest' the finds.

The sea is constantly sorting the items on the seabed by density or by both weight and size. The larger, heavier items will be left behind by the currents, while the lighter, smaller materials will be carried further.

*Around a closed bay where waves travel straight in from the sea, there are three main areas where objects can be found.*

Perhaps the most graphic British example of this is Chesil Beach, Dorset, which stretches for 28km from Portland in the east to Bridport in the west. It well demonstrates the clockwise travel of the currents around the British Isles. The tides and currents have graded the pebbles from as big as 30cm in diameter at the Portland end down to 8–10mm at the Bridport end. There is a gradual and linear grading of the pebble size and weight between each end of the beach.

During the research for this book I talked to some of the older fishermen in West Bay harbour at Bridport. These men had spent their youth in small fishing boats in Lyme Bay and they related how, in the days before electronic instruments, if the sea mist came down and they were unsure of their exact location they would sail due north until they could hear the surf on Chesil Beach. They would listen to the note the pebbles were making as the sea rolled them against one another: a deep note for the large pebbles at the east end and a high-pitched note for the small pebbles at the west end of the beach at Bridport.

Their experience enabled them to judge their position along the beach by the particular note the pebbles were making.

On every foreshore and in every bay in the world this effect is taking place to a greater or lesser extent. Look, learn and log all the information on your regular beaches and you will definitely have the edge over the casual detectorists who may visit.

## WHAT'S THE CHANCE OF FINDING SOMETHING VALUABLE?

A theory I heard many years ago goes something like this. A typical seaside season in Britain will span about four months or sixteen weeks (although the season will be considerably longer in countries with a hotter climate, such as Spain). This gives a conservative figure of 110 days as a season. Now take the fact that the majority of British seaside resorts were created by the Victorians following the building of the railways, say a period of 100 years. This gives a total of 11,000 days during which the beaches could have been busy with visitors.

The theory goes on to assume that each day one person on the busy beach will lose an item of gold jewellery. If we take a typical small wedding band as weighing 3 grams, this gives us a total of 33,000 grams or 330kg of gold laying somewhere below the surface of the beach. Of course, we must consider that the gold we find will not be pure, but will be a mixture of 9, 14, 18 and 22 carats and that the net amount in weight of pure 24ct gold will be less when it is melted down by the bullion house.

I am writing this book at a time when gold has reached a mind-boggling $1,000 an ounce (world markets use the ounce as the weight measure and the US dollar as the currency on the world commodity market). This gives the possibility of finding around $1,000,000 of gold on some of our busiest beaches. Multiply this by the number of busy beaches around the coasts of Britain and Europe and you have an extremely large amount of gold waiting to be found. So to answer the question – yes, the chances of a detectorist finding something of value are really quite high.

# PRIME BEACH DETECTING SPOTS

The wonderful thing about beaches is that they are constantly being replenished with fresh coins, artefacts and, alas, junk. The high season brings thousands seeking the sun. Inevitably they will lose things as a coin or piece of jewellery drops onto the sand without a sound and rapidly sinks out of sight.

In the introduction to this book I said I would demonstrate how a lucrative return could be had if you knew why and where to detect on

the beach. Yet of those out detecting that I have spoken to, few have admitted to giving much thought to why they find items where they do.

Let's take a look at what actually happens on the beaches in the various countries I visit, the items that are lost on them and how local culture and customs, and the behaviour of visiting tourists, can dramatically affect the type and quantity of finds along the beaches and foreshore.

## England

Most visitors to British beaches are day-trippers, arriving from a B&B, hotel, camp site or by car. Only a small percentage of the population live near the beaches and typically they don't use them. Our weather is rarely hotter than 'shorts and sandals', so people have pockets and pockets mean money, which can be dropped while sitting or lying on the sand. Young men nowadays tend to wear swimming shorts and they too have pockets.

British beaches have plenty of concession stands, donkey rides and chair hire points. So there is a need to have cash with you during the time spent on the beach.

As a nation both men and women tend to wear a reasonable amount of jewellery, and few remove it before going on the beach or foreshore. Since not many councils use beach cleaning machines, items remain lost in the sand.

Beaches are generally occupied between about 10am and 6pm. In high summer, however, it will not go dark until after 10pm and it will be light early in the morning. This gives the detectorist a reasonable period of at least four hours at each end of the day to get out detecting.

A word of warning: do not detect on any beaches in any country when they are occupied by the public. Nothing is more likely to get on peoples' nerves when they are there to relax with their family and friends, than persons with a detector grubbing about around them. Use the time when the beach is occupied, instead, by doing some public relations for the hobby by distributing leaflets for your 'Free Finds Service'.

I always make sure that staff on the beach, such as the car park attendants, lifeguards and concession-stand holders, have a leaflet on my service. Many of those I have been able to help by recovering items lost on the beach first heard about me through a recommendation by the beach staff. This again helps the image of the hobby and increases the number of those within my network who can help to find me private land on which I can detect.

### France

Unlike England, the national holiday season in France is sharply defined. It commences on 1 July and finishes on 31 August each year. This system was established after the Second World War in an effort to help the French nation become commercially competitive. The upside to this for the detectorist is that the beaches are deserted for the rest of the year and yet by our standards their weather can be very good out of season.

France does not have a beach bar culture or many concession stands on its beaches. Instead there are street cafés and promenade bars overlooking the beaches. The French are also a great nation for eating outdoor, and extended families can often be seen enjoying home-prepared food and local wine on the beach or under the shade of the pine trees that back many of the beaches on both the Atlantic and Mediterranean coasts.

If we look at their beachwear, we can see an immediate difference in that French men wear swimming trunks: in fact, on many beaches and

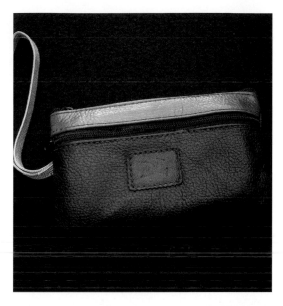

*In France men tend to carry a bag to hold their money, keys and mobile phone, so very little cash is dropped on French beaches compared with those in Spain, for example.*

in a large proportion of the swimming pools it is mandatory to wear trunks rather than swimming shorts. This, of course, means they have no pockets and therefore no money can be dropped.

The French also have a culture of men carrying purses for their keys and money or handbags for all their loose possessions. We can see that the ability to drop money and other items is dramatically reduced in France.

I had been detecting in France for many years before I came to understand why my finds of gold had never amounted to as much in terms of weight. If we look at the build of French men and women, as a race they are slight or slender by nature. It therefore follows that the diameter of any rings found in France will be smaller than those found in such countries as England, Germany and Spain, where the people tend to

*While the beach machines almost turn the sand into talcum powder, they definitely don't collect all the money.*

be of a heavier build. It follows that if you place a gold ring on a petite finger it does not need to be very heavy or wide to be in balance with the finger. These points are reflected in the fact that a typical gold ring found in France will weigh about 1.5 grams, whereas one found in Spain, for example, might average 3.5 grams or more. The same principle follows for gold chains; they are finer and more delicate than those found in other countries.

One added benefit for the detectorist is that there are literally hundreds of leisure lakes throughout the country. Many of these have a beach of imported fine sea sand laid over a membrane and, of course, no tides. The local tourist office will have details of the lakes in the area you may be visiting.

My experience is that the 'Free Finds Service' is well received in France and it provides a useful contact point with the public, though of course it helps if you can speak some French.

## Spain

Spain is without doubt the best and most productive country for metal detecting I have ever visited, an observation that has been confirmed over the many years I have been visiting there.

Spain is Europe's number one destination for beach holidays, receiving in excess of 60 million visitors each year. The majority of these will visit the Costas or coast. Its weather means that, during the arid high season, the consistent high temperatures and daily cleaning of the beaches by machines that froth up the top surface result in an extremely soft beach.

There is a well-developed tapas/beach bar culture. Many of the beach bars are owned by the local town council. Typically they are a variety of designer portacabin, placed on the beach for the season and rented out for a fixed fee. They all conform to a fixed design, which means that the kitchen facilities, toilets and so on are of a good standard.

The resort of Jávea (or Xàbia in Catalan), north of Benidorm on the Costa Blanca, has a stretch of beach about 2km long where there were eleven bars actually on the foreshore with lots of tables and chairs spread out around them. Most of these bars are open from 1 June until the end of the schools' half-term holiday around mid-October. This gives a season of about 140 days, 30 per cent longer than in Britain. During June, July and August they are often open for 24 hours a day.

The life of a bar over a 24 hour period looks something like this. The young people will be there partying and drinking all night. When they go home the bar staff clear up and restock before the families come down to the beach for the day, followed by the older people promenading and stopping for their coffee and brandy in the evening. By late evening the young people are

back and the cycle starts all over again. Bear in mind that people drinking late into the night become less particular in their handling of money, the only light on the tables is candlelight, and so any money that is dropped is long gone.

One of the bar owners on the beach at Jávea confirmed that his bar can average about 3,000 Euros a day during the high season, meaning that up to 500,000 Euros may change hands during the season. Much of it is handed to the waiters to pay for drinks and food at the tables out on the sand. Of course, if any money gets dropped it instantly disappears down into the fine dry sand, to await the detectorist.

As much as 300 Euros has been recovered by the author and his wife from around just one of these bars based out on the sand. This is not a one-off-occurrence, but something that has

*During the season bars are open almost all hours.*

*There can be rich pickings when the sand sculptors have finished at the end of the season, since many of the coins that people throw into their collecting buckets end up in the sand.*

been repeated over and over again in our years of detecting in Spain.

Spain's other highly developed beach businesses are able to operate all along the Mediterranean coast due entirely to the small tides mentioned above. The effect of these small tides on the commercial operations is that they can take place on what to all intents and purposes is a lake. This provides the concessions with a static waterline from which they can operate hire businesses for jet-skis, pedalos, dinghies, canoes, waterskiing, windsurfing and paragliding. To this can be added pleasure boat and glass-bottomed boat trips, African pedlars selling their ethnic wares and, naturally, sunbeds and parasols for hire. All of these operations are handling money out on the sand, with the inevitable results that coins will end up lost.

A Spanish newspaper article estimated that the cash turnover of all the concessions and bars on Benidorm beach is in the region of 250,000 Euros per day. This is admittedly one of the busiest beaches in Spain, but it is still a huge amount of money to be handled on a sandy surface.

If you see sand sculptors on the beach, make a careful note of precisely where they operate because in the low season, when they have gone away, there will always be coins to be found from donations that were thrown at the bowl but missed.

In recent years the Spanish authorities have put a lot of effort into landscaping their beaches. You can now find palm groves planted on the beach to add some greenery and provide shade. Families, especially those with young children, often spread themselves out in these areas, so they are well worth searching when no one is there.

If we look at the swimwear seen on Spanish beaches, the universal appeal to the men of swimming shorts or Bermuda shorts is immediately apparent. This is due to several factors:

- Most people stay in apartments within walking distance of the beach. During the long hot summers, the men don't want to walk to the beach and then have to change, so they wear swimming shorts.
- Beach bars require shorts or sarongs to be worn when using their facilities.
- Because of the bars and beach entertainment on offer, the men have to wear shorts with pockets as they need cash to be available.
- The majority are there for one or two weeks and are after a good time. Common

sense is left at home along with their cares and worries, so they often carry more change in their pockets than they would back home.

- Most couples and families rent a pair of sunbeds and a parasol for the day and use it as a base. Their clothes, bags or other belongings will be grouped together on the sand in these areas. Inevitably things will get lost when picking up trousers, skirts or shorts, for example, and it is easy for items to fall out of pockets and into the sand. Finds have included money, jewellery, both gold and silver, and even paper money in a discarded cigarette packet.

During the season there are more than 500 sunbeds for hire on the beach at Jávea, costing 10 Euros per pair per day. The beds are cleared away every evening, so this is the time to get out

*Don't ignore a good signal just because it looks wrong. Believe what your detector is saying.*

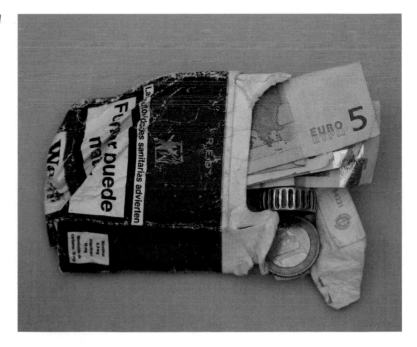

*A total of 1,360 Euros: not many hobbies are as profitable.*

detecting, as the beaches are floodlit all night. If you choose to go out in the morning you would need to make a very early start, since by 7.30am the boys are putting the beds out again ready for another day's hire.

When I give talks on metal detecting, there always seems to be someone in the audience who says, 'Yes, yes, OK. So all of this money is supposed to be lost, but do you really find anything?' Well, the answer is a resounding 'Yes':

over eight weeks in Spain in 2008 we found 1,360 Euros on the beaches, plus what I found in the water, but that story can wait until later.

> **Study your beaches, keep a log, take photos. Knowledge is power, reap the rewards.**

# CHAPTER 13

# SAFETY AND EQUIPMENT FOR UNDERWATER DETECTING

Water presents its own range of dangers. Where you may get a second chance on land after a minor slip or accident, in the water a similar occurrence can rapidly turn into a frightening and possibly fatal situation. Never underestimate the power of water. A fireman has told me that he isn't frightened of fire – you can fight it with water – but no one can check water if it is out of control.

Check the tide tables and plan your trip accordingly. This point is so important that I make no excuse for repeating myself. You can see from tide charts that the tide does not just go in and out, in a symmetrical pattern, as many people imagine.

Lack of clear understanding of the tide tables can be extremely dangerous. In certain areas around the coast, the water, when the tide turns, will come up the beach faster than a man can run. Let me give you a sombre example of what happens when you disregard safety around the water.

I also enjoy sea fishing and my 'local' coast is the Bristol Channel from the first Severn Bridge down to Burnham-on-Sea, a dangerous stretch with the second biggest rise and fall of tide in the world (more than 17m). In a recent incident, a local man, fishing on his own, was washed away as the tide turned and started to come in.

The water rises very quickly, initially by 1.2m in 20 minutes. He had been fishing from a shingle spit that projects out into the channel under the Severn Bridge and is exposed at low tide. The incident report makes no mention of him wearing a flotation suit or life jacket, but it does say he was wearing a camouflage jacket and chest waders, a dangerous combination that cost him his life.

The moral is clear: *never* go near the water unless you understand the profile of the tidal flow, have a detailed weather forecast and are properly equipped, dressed and prepared in every way. In addition, *never* go without a reliable 'buddy'. Even if he or she is not a detectorist they can at least keep an eye out for you and raise the alarm quickly if needed.

## EQUIPMENT FOR USE IN WATER

### *The Metal Detector*

As mentioned in Chapter 2, the detectors for use in and under the water are highly specialized pieces of equipment, able to cope with the extreme environment encountered in shallow water surf detecting and the high pressures experienced when used at depths of up to 30m (100ft) by detectorists who are diving. These detectors have to operate in salt water which may be at temperatures down to 5 or 6 degrees and will be operating in a cloud of silt once the recovery of an artefact is underway. For these reasons it is vital that the detector and all of your other underwater equipment are washed with fresh water as soon as possible after every search.

The main difference in the design and construction of underwater detectors is in their waterproofing. Some manufacturers opt for re-sealable opening units giving access to the batteries. A clear example of this approach can be seen with the red silicon 'O ring' which sits within the labyrinth and forms the seal on the control and battery box of the deep-seeking Whites Surfmaster PI Pro

detector. These types of seals should be replaced at least once a year, and more often if the machine is in regular use. It it is a simple job to change the seal, but a seal failure would almost certainly end up in the total destruction of all the electronics in the control box and could result in repairs costing hundreds of pounds.

Another first-class example of an under water detector is the Minelab Excalibur. This is a multi-tone motion detector with 'Broad Band Spectrum', a unique electronic transmission system putting out multiple signals from the coil providing an enhanced search ability. There are two models of the Excalibur available, the 800 and the 1000. The only difference is the size of the search coil, being 8cm and 10cm, respectively.

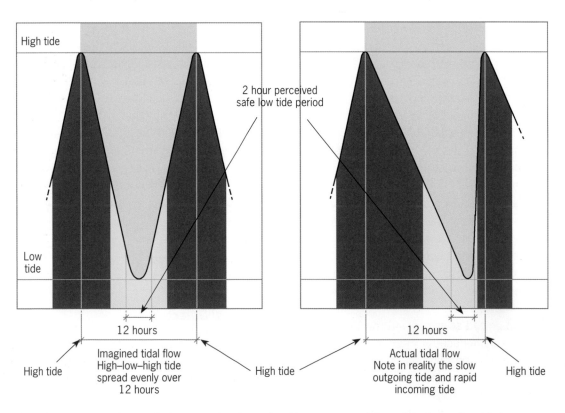

*The tidal flow in the Bristol Channel can be deceptive. Note the rate of flow of the incoming tide in this example.*

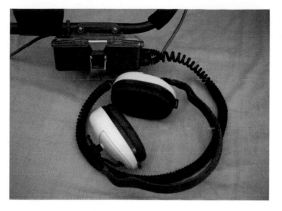

The Whites Surf Master PI underwater detector has a split control/battery box. The side clamps and red 'O ring' provide the mechanical seal against water ingression.

The red 'O ring' sits in the top half of control box labyrinth. All underwater detectors have permanently wired waterproof headphones.

Waterproof connector

The Minelab Excalibur underwater detector has a sealed control unit and a sealed rechargeable battery unit. These are connected by a waterproof three-pin screw plug.

This close-up of the battery connector plug on the Excalibur clearly shows the neoprene seal; if you have one, you should smear a little silicon grease on this seal.

Minelab have taken a different approach to battery and control box sealing. They have opted for a sealed rechargeable battery pack rather than the replaceable alkali-type batteries other manufacturers use. The control box is also a sealed unit and so the chance of water ingress problems is reduced in the Minelab design. The only area the detectorist must pay close attention to is the waterproof battery/control box connection: this must be clean and grit free, remembering that silt is present when you are detecting underwater.

I regularly use an Excalibur 1000 and find it better to apply a smear of silicon grease on the plug to ensure a perfect seal each time the battery is refitted after charging.

## Clothing

The equipment you use for underwater detecting needs to be correct and designed for the task in hand. A detecting magazine from the mid-1980s carried an article about a detectorist who, for safety reasons, made holes in his Wellingtons.

This was to enable any water that came over the top of them while he was wading in the surf to also get out, ensuring they didn't drag him down into the water. I had to check that the magazine wasn't dated 1 April: I hope things like this would not get printed nowadays.

Wetsuits, boots and gloves all need to be designed for use in the sea or freshwater conditions you will be working in. Boots, for example, need to be diver's boots, not wind surfing or dinghy sailing boots, as these will have no reinforcing in the soles. Gloves also need to be of a type with Kevlar outer protection.

Some publications recommend the use of waders for shallow water detecting. I would *never* advocate the use of waders. I repeat, if they fill with water they are lethal. If you insist on wearing waders, the only type with any element of safety are the tight-fitting ones in neoprene. These are in effect three-quarters of a wet suit, but I still think you would be much safer in a full wet suit.

*Always be aware of your safety when working in deep water and make sure you can be seen.*

I use a range of three wet suits in three different thicknesses: 3mm, 5mm and 10mm. They come with short sleeves and legs or long. To these are added neoprene socks, gloves and boots. Which pattern I use, or combination of them, depends on the water temperature, the wind strength and the ambient temperature.

Even when detecting on a hot day in Spain, with an air temperature of 25 to 28 degrees, a sea temperature of 20 degrees and a wind speed of 50km/h, I still feel the wind chill on my upper body as I go in and out of the deep water following a gridiron search pattern. Under these conditions I may well need a 5mm suit.

When detecting in one of the hundreds of freshwater lakes in France, often known as a *base de loisir* ('leisure site'), even on a hot day the 10mm suit can be required to combat the low water temperature of these lakes. Since they are often fed by mountain streams, a water temperature as low as 10 degrees is not uncommon. If the weather becomes overcast and windy, particularly in October or November, you can wear a 3mm neoprene tee-shirt underneath a 10mm suit for extra insulation.

Always wear a fluorescent cap, or at least a light coloured one, when you are in the water. You may be in up to your shoulders at times and it can be difficult for other water users to see you. Take no chances but follow the rule 'be seen, be safe'. It is your responsibility to make yourself aware of the water sports that may be going on where you intend to detect. These can include pedalos, dingy sailing, windsurfing, jet-skiing and even speedboats towing waterskiers. Frequently people may have only rented the equipment and have had little training or experience using it. Always be willing to leave and detect somewhere else if you feel your safety may be compromised.

A strong diver's knife is an essential piece of kit.

## Personal equipment

The personal equipment you carry with you will be similar to that used when detecting inland, although it follows that some of it will need to be in waterproof containers, such as the first aid kit and mobile phone. Any tools or knives you need should be made of stainless steel, as saltwater will soon corrode and ruin mild steel items.

The knife you carry should be a good quality diver's knife. These are very strong and have a saw edge on one side of the blade and a good cutting edge on the other. A penknife or such is not up to the job.

The need for a good quality knife was brought home to me while detecting in a river estuary on the Atlantic coast of southwest France. I had been detecting with the ebbing tide. When the tide reached its lowest point, I started to work backwards and forwards in a long gully in about 1m of water. As the tide turned I began to work back up the beach with the tide. With the water level rising, I encountered a problem that could easily have been very dangerous. I had become entangled in a discarded mooring rope and couldn't free myself. I shouted to my detecting 'buddy', but it can be difficult to hear when wearing ear defender-type headphones. I blew fiercely on the 'police whistle' worn on a lanyard around my neck and then started to cut the rope with my diver's knife. After my 'buddy' arrived it still took about ten minutes for the two of us, working together, to cut through the rope and set me free.

A possible disaster was avoided by using the 'buddy system', working as a team, having the right tools to hand and keeping calm.

One further piece of equipment I would recommend for use in an estuary or open sea conditions is a semi-automatic life jacket that folds up when not in use and provides a warm collar around the neck. Models are available that incorporate a location beacon and strobe light. Some detectorists see this as overkill, but I would advise taking every step possible to ensure your safety.

> Safety first. There is no second chance in and around water.

# CHAPTER 14

# UNDERWATER DETECTING

I freely admit that underwater detecting is my passion. There are several reasons for this.

As a keen sea fisherman, I owned a fishing boat for many years before I started metal detecting. I was always captivated by the thought of there being treasure in the sea as well as fish. When waiting for the fish to bite we would often wonder what might be down there just waiting to be found. Part of my enjoyment in sea fishing came from planning the trips and keeping a log of all of the tides, weather, sea conditions, baits used and fish caught. I would spend hours pouring over charts and studying tidal flows, seabed contours and sea temperatures. It wasn't just a fishing trip, it was hunting and I had to work out my tactics to catch the biggest fish possible. Underwater detecting has many similarities, especially if you want to locate big finds.

Being partially disabled I find it difficult to walk on fields, although I cope better on beaches with firm sand where my bad leg can find its own angle of support. When I first tried underwater detecting it was as though I had had a leg transplant. The pleasure of being able to walk about in the water with the buoyancy of the wetsuit taking the weight off my leg is a fantastic experience that I wholeheartedly recommend to any detectorist with a similar disability.

Shallow water detecting, the variant described here, can be carried out around much of the Mediterranean and the Adriatic, as well as in Europe's many inland lakes, owing to the small tidal variation (or, in the case of the lakes, none at all). This means that, unlike around the British Isles or along the Atlantic coasts of France, Spain and Portugal, the water line on the beaches is more or less static.

Where you have a tidal movement similar that along the Atlantic coasts, underwater detecting is really only needed below the Spring Tides low water mark. On these types of beaches the majority of the sea area in which people swim and play will be uncovered as the tide goes out twice a day. Coins and artefacts that have been dropped can be recovered using the beach detecting methods (see Chapter 12).

## BEACH BEHAVIOUR

It is a useful observation to compare the activities of people when they are in the water at Mediterranean resorts with how the public use the water at British resorts. After the size of the tides, the single biggest difference between the areas is the ambient temperature. In the UK we experience summer temperatures of typically around 20 degrees (should we be fortunate). On Mediterranean beaches, however, temperatures of 40 degrees in the shade are quite normal in high summer, while on the open beach in the direct sun a temperature of 65 degrees or more may be reached.

People in 1.5m of water     Beach bar     Boat/pedalo hire

*Many people go into the water to cool down rather than to swim.*

People on British beaches mainly use the water for a swim, to play games or 'take a quick dip'. Abroad I have noticed that, while some go into the water for a swim, the vast majority go in to cool down and often spend up to an hour at a time just standing or bobbing up and down in shoulder deep water. Many others sit in the shallow water with just their head and shoulders out of the water.

The effect of spending this amount of time in the water, as we all know, is for your hands and fingers to shrink and become rather wrinkled due to the beginnings of hypothermia. These are the same hands that were used to apply suntan oil back on the beach, causing rings and bracelets to slip off with remarkable ease. People sitting in the water are often seen running their hands through the sand on the seabed. Again it is very easy to lose a ring, bracelet or watch while doing this. Once a piece of jewellery has come off it disappears instantly and no amount of running your hands through the sand will help you find it. You will only make it sink further down.

The reason you find coins in the sea along the Spanish Mediterranean coast is that the men wear swimming shorts and carry money to use in the bars and other beach concessions (see Chapter 12). When they sit down in the water the pockets are horizontal and it is very easy for coins to fall out. Those who stand in deeper water bobbing up and down are just as likely to jog coins out of their pockets. Add in those who are playing games, duck diving and doing handstands in the water and it is no wonder that there is so much gold, silver and coins to be found. It is not unknown to have to come out of the water to empty my finds pouch partway through a session because it is full to capacity.

It is not just the value of the coins. It is their sheer quantity. A recent holiday produced a total haul of nearly 2,000 Euros. It was a surprise to look at them in a different way and count the actual numbers – more than 6,100 individual coins. Whichever way you look at it, that's an awful lot of holes to dig.

*As can be seen in this view of a partially drained lake in France, most people will gather between the driftwood line and water line seen here, when the lake is full of water in high season, making it a prime detecting zone.*

### Lakes

On the type of beaches created around lakes, while the sand can be moved around by the wind and weather, artefacts more or less stay where they are dropped. This is because lake beaches are largely unaffected by wave action.

The same applies to such as coins or jewellery lost in the water of the lakes. During the winter waves are created during high winds or storms, allowing items to sink lower into the silt, but there are no currents in the lakes to move articles around. This gives the underwater detectorist the opportunity to start a search by immediately adopting the double gridiron search pattern (see Chapter 4). This type of search will offer the best chance of recovering any finds in the area of the lake most used by people to swim or play.

Owing to the way people spend their time in the water, there is little point in detecting past the maximum wading depth. However you must cover from the very edge of the waterline on the beach out to the deepest you possibly can.

## COASTAL BAYS

When you first arrive at a new bay on the coast, select two landmarks on the beach and a single point out at sea or on the horizon; this could be a buoy, a prominent feature or a distant mountain peak. These will form the boundary markers for your search pattern. Do not be too ambitious with the size of your area as it is hard work wading in the water swinging a detector back and forth. In a new bay the first search pattern to try is the envelope pattern (see Chapter 4). This pattern helps to give you a feel for the shape of the seabed and identify any trenches or gullies the currents have scoured out. Having completed this search, analyse whatever finds you have recovered and what you have learned of the seabed. While you take a break from the water, make a preliminary map of the bay, including any features on the seabed and the position of the finds and what type they are.

At this stage always look for any hotspots (areas of multiple finds) and for any features on the seabed. Depending on what shows up, choose a hotspot or gully and then carry out a gridiron search pattern targeting this area rather than the whole bay. From first arriving at the bay to completing this evaluation and search may take about four or five hours, which is probably enough for one session. The next stage is to bring the map up to date and then decide whether the next day you should:

- carry out further search patterns on other areas within the bay, or
- carry out some double gridiron searches on areas that showed up as hotspots.

If you are lucky enough to find one or more hotspots, make sure you can return to them again in the future. Hotspot locations are an invaluable resource for any detectorist. I know of certain hotspots in France and Spain that have each yielded as many as two or three hundred items over the years. In order to achieve these results you must be able to return to their *exact* location. Take bearings of prominent landmarks with a compass and log them on your map. Make sure you pick features that are likely to be there when you next visit, such as towers, lampposts and buildings. Buoys in the sea can get brought in during the winter months or moved by stormy weather. Even large trees can get

felled. Be warned, take care not to lose a good hotspot.

The skills you initially learned by concentrating and learning the language of your detector (see Chapter 4) are vitally important when underwater detecting. Because you are unable to physically 'see' the seabed, it is necessary to build up a clear mental picture of what is beneath the surface. Learn to use all of your senses to understand what is happening when in the water. Even the smallest hump or depression in the seabed, for example, must be felt with your feet. Does the seabed slope from left to right or right to left? Is it going down and deeper or up and shallower? Can you feel the current on your legs and body, in which direction is it travelling and how strong is it? You may well find that, when trying to get the very most out of the machine and increase your concentration, it is better to close your eyes.

All of the information in this chapter is not much use unless you also know how to recover your finds. On the beach, as we have seen, it is not too difficult to locate the item, carefully dig the target out and recover it using a sand scoop. In shallow water the recovery system is largely the same: dig the item out from the seabed with a backhoe or similar tool, and then use the sand scoop so that the sand and water can drain out leaving the find behind.

What do you do, however, once you cannot bend down without your head going underwater? From this point, out to your maximum wading depth, is an area that holds some of the richest finds, so how do you recover the target signals?

For this you need a digging tool that will enable you to dig down into the seabed, possibly to a depth of 40cm if you are using a PI detector, then collect a target item securely and then enable you to raise it to the surface single-handed,

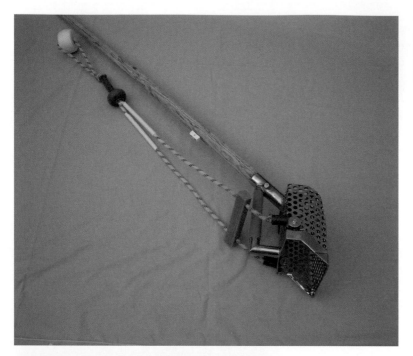

*The author's own design of digging tool: hold the handle away from you and dig straight down into the sand.*

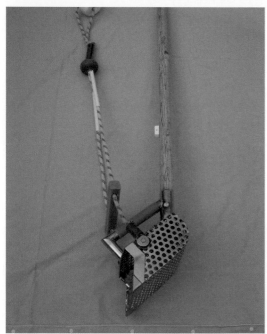

*Now pull the handle towards you and continue to lever it down to the seabed behind you.*

rinsing out the sand and gravel while allowing the find to remain in the scoop. All of this should be carried out while standing in 1.4m of water or more.

There are four functions such a tool has to perform:

- ▪ Dig
- ▪ Collect
- ▪ Raise
- ▪ Rinse

After trying several commercial alternatives I decided to make my own. My inspiration came from watching a ditching excavator at work on nearby farmland and performing the same four actions that the underwater digger had to carry out. The main difference between the excavator I was watching and a digger you would see working on a building site was that the ditching excavator had a mesh bucket, allowing the

*With your foot initially placed on the scoop, pull up on the floating rope to retrieve it and the contents of the scoop will be rinsed as the water drains through the holes.*

water to drain away. A digger-shaped bucket of mesh type construction would provide the solution; it would dig, collect and rinse, but how could I easily raise it to the surface? The answer eventually turned out to be floating rope.

As can be seen in the accompanying photographs, the bucket is a standard JCB digger shape and is made from laser-profiled stainless steel of a marine grade. It is mounted at an angle of 45 degrees on the end of a hickory handle shaft, which should continue to last for many years in and out of seawater. The attached floating rope is always available at or just below the surface of the water and enables the digger to be recovered single-handed. I have experienced no problems with the design during the five years that I have used it for detecting abroad. It is covered by registered design rights.

A place where you go to get money is called a bank. I think it should be called a sandbank.

# CHAPTER 15

# CLEANING AND PRESENTING FINDS

Finding an interesting or valuable artefact is without doubt an exciting experience. It's what our hobby is about. But the sight of a beautiful artefact that has been carefully cleaned, restored and put on display can be an equally stimulating experience.

I am not an envious person by nature, but whenever I visit Swindon Museum and look at two significant finds made by the same detectorist on display in their respective cases with his name on them, I wish that some of my finds were as historically significant and could be cleaned and presented as professionally. (For more about these finds, see Chapter 16.)

The cleaning of finds can be divided into two categories:

- Modern finds: money, jewellery, watches and so on, predominantly found in parks, on the beach or in the water.
- Historic finds: old coins and artefacts of historic value found mainly in the soil on agricultural land.

The methods for handling and treating articles from these two groups during the cleaning process could not be more different.

## CLEANING MODERN FINDS

This is by some way the more straightforward category. For the purpose of this book, modern money is coinage in current circulation. In the countries covered here that is Sterling or Euro coins as used in the various countries of the European Union. Modern jewellery that is recovered comes predominantly from lakes and the sea, and falls into the categories of gold, silver, platinum, titanium and stainless steel. The last two of these are used in the making of modern designs mainly bought by young people.

If the recovered coins have been in the water for some time in an area where the sea or lake bed is heavily mineralized with traces of metals, they will be covered in a coating of those metals and silt.

The coastal region of Murcia in Spain, for example, has copper and lead mines that date back at least to Roman times. Spoil from these mines has found its way into the sea. The minute metal particles adhere to the coins by electrolysis, resulting from the presence of warm saline water and an abundance of sunshine. This effectively 'copper plates' or 'lead coats' the coins. The top row of coins in the accompanying photograph demonstrates the results. Since the coating can

*Three stages in cleaning coins: (top) as found; (middle) first clean; (bottom) final polish.*

be quite dense, the first thing to do is to sort the coins into the various types of coatings that they have acquired since they were buried; in this instance that would be copper-coated, lead-coated and general corrosion or encrustation.

It is most important to clean these various groups separately. Failure to observe this will result in cross-contamination of the deposits on the coins. The results can be exceedingly difficult to remove.

## Equipment for Cleaning Modern Cash Finds

The most important and useful piece of equipment for cleaning modern coins is a barrelling machine. These were originally manufactured for polishing semi-precious stones for use in the making of jewellery. It did not take the metal detectorists very long, however, to recognize the role they could play in their hobby. The machine consists of a 100mm diameter plastic barrel, which is about 150mm long and has a

removable lid at each end. The barrel sits on a pair of rollers, one of which is driven by an electric motor via a geared drive belt. When the power is turned on the barrel rotates at between 20 to 50rpm, depending on the load placed in the barrel.

*A hard-worked barrel cleaning machine.*

*Steel shapes used during the first clean. The steel wood screws can be plainly be seen.*

Other items needed as part of this cleaning kit include about 500 grams of steel shot, an old towel (cleaning detector finds is a messy job), an old washing-up bowl and a sieve (perhaps an old flour sieve). You will also require washing-up liquid and, for the final polishing, a fine and gentle abrasive such as crushed nut husks or a polishing product such as Walsh's Barrel Brite.

For information about H. S. Walsh & Sons Ltd and on specialized companies based in the Jewellery Quarter of Birmingham, see Useful Contacts.

## Cleaning Modern Coins

*British Coins*

British coinage issued since the Second World War does not contain any silver, but instead uses cupro-nickel. For cleaning purposes it may divided into two groups:

- 2 pound, 1 pound, 50 pence, 20 pence, 10 pence and 5 pence coins
- 2 pence and 1 pence coins, currently made from iron and then copper nickel-coated.

*Euro Coins*

When the euro was introduced in January 2001, all the existing currencies were withdrawn over the following two months, a massive logistical problem that went surprisingly smoothly. As with British coins, they may be divided into two groups:

- 2 euro, 1 euro, 50 cents, 20 cents and 10 cents pieces, made from cupro-nickel
- 5 cent, 2 cent and 1 cent coins, made from iron coated with copper nickel.

*Cleaning Process*

The first process in the cleaning cycle is to load the barrel with the steel shapes, which are used as the scouring agent. Following many years of experimenting I have concluded that the best things to use for this initial clean are steel wood screws mixed with commercially available steel shot. After the steel shapes have been placed in the barrel, add approximately 500 grams of the coins to be cleaned, as you do so checking one last time that no copper nickel coins have got mixed in (or they will coat everything in copper). Cover the contents of the barrel with lukewarm water, then introduce a small amount of washing-up liquid (enough to cover a fingernail is ample). Secure the lid onto the barrel. Now press the centre and lift the outer edge of the lid to release any air inside the barrel. If you do not do this, the barrel will become pressurized and the water will leak out.

Switch on and allow the barrelling machine to come up to speed. Dry the barrel with an old towel and then place it on the rollers. Some assistance in getting it up to speed will help ease the initial load on the motor. Leave the rig to run for about two hours. Don't worry about the running costs, since the motor uses only about as much electricity as a small light bulb.

When it is time stop the machine, take the barrel and remove the lid while holding it over the washing-up bowl. Do be careful not to get any of the slurry over yourself or anything else as it is likely to make a stain that may be almost impossible to remove. Now empty the contents of the barrel into the sieve. Hold the sieve over the bowl and under a running tap to rinse off everything and discard the slurry. The coins will look similar to those in the middle row in the photograph.

It is now time for the final polish. To achieve this, put the steel shapes and the coins back into the barrel. Half fill the barrel with warm water and add one dessertspoon of Barrel Brite, put the lid on, following the previous instructions to

exclude air from the barrel, and return it to the machine as previously described. Run the machine for two hours and then check to see if the coins are polished satisfactorily. If they are not return everything to the barrel and repeat the procedure. Experience will teach you how long is required to remove each type of contamination. When finished the coins will look like those on the bottom row. The procedures are repeated for each group of metals (copper bronze and cupronickel) and also for each type of contamination. Do not mix them. It is very difficult to remove and shops and banks do not want 'copper 50 pence pieces'.

### Cleaning Modern Jewellery

The process for cleaning modern silver jewellery is exactly the same as for modern coins except that I use the steel shot and omit the steel wood screws from the barrel. This provides a gentler cleaning action for rings, chains, bracelets and pendants. The effect of sulphide, the grey/black coating that covers anything made of silver that you find underwater, can be seen on the rings on the top row of the photograph on page 128. It may well take up to two hours to dislodge all the sulphide. When this has been done, remove the contents from the barrel, separate the steel shot from the jewellery and wash everything off. Return the jewellery to the barrel with only fresh water and a measure of Barrel Brite, and tumble the contents for a further two hours. This will impart everything with an incredibly good polished surface. Remove all the items and rinse in warm water, drying them off with a towel. They will then look like the rings on the bottom row.

Gold needs hardly any cleaning, no matter how long it has been in the water, although there may be some discoloration on the soldered joints within the items of jewellery. Decide which

## JEWELLERY MAKING USING FINDS MADE WITH METAL DETECTORS

*Pete Hyams polishing the ring in his well-equipped workshop.*

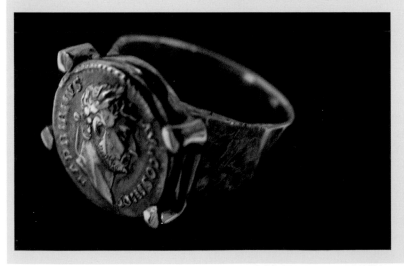

*The completed 'Roman' ring looking most authentic. (Peter Hyams)*

One of my friends, whose detecting exploits may be found in Chapter 16, has branched out in a new direction and enrolled on a professional jewellery-making course offered in Birmingham's Jewellery Quarter. Students who complete the ten-week course, spread over two years, become qualified jewellers. This has required the purchase of a quantity of specialist tools and equipment. His background as an electrical engineer has equipped him with the appropriate hand skills to learn this new trade.

His particular interest lies in making copies of ancient artefacts, mainly Celtic, Roman and Saxon brooches and rings, and some of his pieces are extraordinarily good. One of the most attractive is a replica of a Roman ring made from 9ct gold. It was cast in a mould using cuttlefish bone and then hand finished. The coin set in it is a genuine Roman denarius.

He recently made a ring for my wife using the diamonds from a ring I found while detecting underwater in Spain. The original ring was rather chunky and she wanted something more feminine. We saw the sort of design she wanted in a jeweller's window in Albi on the return journey and took a photograph.

*This 18-carat gold ring, set with 1 carat of diamonds, was found when detecting underwater (Eileen Coe).*

*The finished ring created by resetting diamonds from one ring into another. (Ring by Pete Hyams; photo by Brian Cavill)*

2290 €

*The ring design spotted in a jeweller's window in France.*

I later showed my friend the ring I had found and the photograph. After discussing the project with his tutor, it was decided to remove the stones, which were each one-third of a carat and 4.5mm in diameter, and get a new 18ct white gold claw setting and a yellow 18ct saddle ring to hold the completed setting. The finished ring was then hallmarked for Sue and has been much admired.

*Silver rings recovered from the sea, before and after cleaning.*

pieces of gold jewellery need barrel cleaning, since it would be advisable to omit this process for items set with stones.

For gold items you intend to barrel clean the process is similar to that for the final phase of cleaning silver. Put the gold, warm water and a tablespoon of Barrel Brite into the cleaning barrel and let it work away for about one hour. This is normally plenty of time for gold to be cleaned and polished.

Following barrel cleaning, it may be thought beneficial to polish the jewellery further with something like a high-speed Dremel polishing machine and 'jeweller's rouge'. Great care must be taken not to damage the items. Since everyone's hand skills will be different, it is difficult to offer general advice. If you wish to take this further, books on polishing and finishing jewellery may be obtained from your local library or detector dealer. It is even possible to go on training courses. Whatever you decide, practise and hone your skills on some of the cheaper silver jewellery that you are bound to find during your searches.

## CLEANING HISTORIC FINDS

The unchallenged golden rule concerning the cleaning of historic finds is, if you have any doubt as to your skills and ability, don't clean the item. You may damage it and ruin its value completely by blundering on with harsh or destructive cleaning methods.

Those actively involved in the cleaning and restoration of any historic items – whether they are coins, artefacts or even historic racing cars – know that there are four stages in any item's appearance:

- What it was like when it was made.
- What it was like when it was used.
- What it was like when it was found.
- What it is like after it is cleaned or restored.

We can theorize about the first two stages and perhaps by research we can gain a good idea of what the items were like during these periods. The third condition is unique, because it is precisely what the item was like at that exact moment it was found. No one except you may have set eyes on this artefact for perhaps as long as 2,000 years. It can never return to this condition once cleaning or restoration work commences.

The fourth stage is a creation of the restorer's mind and sometimes bears little relationship to what the article looked like when it was made and used. When I ran a business restoring historic racing cars, I used to deal with two types of clients. The first wanted the car to be restored mechanically so that it could be used on the race track, but with as little external restoration as possible so that the car remained visually original. One client with an ex-works D type Jaguar wanted a dent in the bodywork left alone, because it had been inflicted during the 1957 Le Mans 24-hour race when the car was in its heyday. He was very proud of a photograph showing the car at Le Mans complete with dent. The second type of customer would want a total rebuild from the 'chassis up' including every last nut and bolt. Cars given this treatment were undoubtedly beautiful and it was fantastic to see them out on the track. But they had never been prepared to those standards when they were first made or raced, and were viewed by some critics as re-creations, not restorations.

This anecdote demonstrates that there can be a fine line concerning how far we go in cleaning our finds. Collectors or museums have their own criteria for the preservation of artefacts and they could easily be quite different to yours. Certain collectors are known to mark down the value of coins at the slightest sign of them having chinked together with other coins, so imagine what effect bad cleaning or over-restoration will have on their value.

The consensus among detecting colleagues and contacts at the local museum is that, if you really must clean any coin or artefact you find, you should soak it in warm distilled water and then gently agitate the dirt with a soft bristle toothbrush until it is removed. You may later wish to use a wet cotton bud or a softened cocktail stick to remove any dirt left in nooks or crannies. Never use anything abrasive. This work is best carried out under a magnifying glass or using one of the latest digital hand-held microscopes. The final treatment could be a wipe-over with a lint-free cloth soaked in a little olive oil and buffing it up using a clean lint-free cloth.

## DISPLAYING YOUR FINDS

To display your finds you will need to look at how the professionals do it. For example if the finds you have cleaned and polished are modern jewellery, take a look in a jewellers and see how they display similar items. Rings look much better in a display case than in a pile. Lighting is also important. A ring set with a diamond, for

*This display does not show off these silver rings to their best advantage.*

example, will come alive when lit with a bright halogen spot. Hundreds of different types of commercial jewellery display boxes, trays and general display aids are on offer on eBay.

For historic items you should again look at how the experts do it. Visit your local museum, look at their displays, ask the staff for tips and talk to the Finds Liaison Officer in charge of the Portable Antiquities Scheme, who should plenty of ideas about preserving and presenting your finds. Velvet-lined coin display cases, for example, are available via eBay or through advertisements in detecting magazines. They come in a range of sizes and all of them have dividers, both horizontal

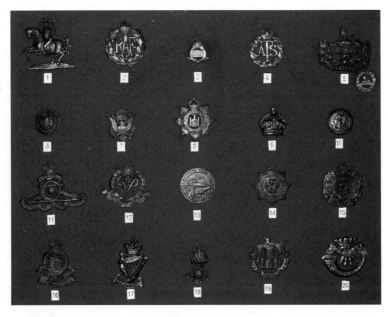

*A good example of military items properly displayed in a purpose-made case. (Find and display by Keith James, photo by Brian Cavill)*

1  Cap badge of the Fife & Forfar Yeomanry 1914, found Wroughton
2  Cap badge of the Royal Air Force, King's Crown, found Blunsden
3  Royal Air Force Volunteer Reserve, Sergeant pilot's silver lapel badge, found Blunsden
4  Auxiliary Territorial Service cap badge, found Blunsden
5  Gloucester Regiment 1914, and back badge, found separately
6  Royal Scots button, found Chiseldon
7  American serviceman's collar badge, World War II, found Chiseldon
8  Cap badge, the Devonshire Regiment, World War II, found Chiseldon
9  King's Crown, Major's epaulette or NCO's sleeve fitting, found Wroughton

10  Button, Gordon Highlanders, found Chiseldon
11  Royal Artillery cap badge, World War II
12  Royal Military Police cap badge, World War II
13  French medallion referring to the Maginot Line defences
14  Royal Army Service Corps cap badge, Officer's bronzed finish, found Blunsden
15  Royal Engineer's cap badge, 1914
16  Royal Army Ordnance Corps cap badge, found Chiseldon
17  Cap badge of the Royal Irish Rifles
18  Royal Artillery beret badge, found Marston Maisey
19  Cap badge 1914, Essex Regiment, found Chiseldon
20  Cap badge 1914, Duke of Cornwall's Light Infantry, found Wroughton

*Long John Silver or Jack Sparrow would have been proud of this.*

and vertical, that prevent the coins touching one another and so preserve their condition.

For artefacts you have found, cleaned and now wish to display there is a useful source of ready-made display frames, available from companies such as the specialist art supply chain HobbyCraft, originally intended for framing découpage pictures and dried flower displays.

Many websites offer display cases suitable for showing off a wide range of finds of all shapes and sizes. Some individuals also have the skills to make their own display cases.

If you wish to be more imaginative you could try a creative approach, using other objects to enhance your finds or set them in a themed display.

> **When it comes to cleaning your finds, the golden rule is, if in doubt, don't.**

# CHAPTER 16
# OUTSTANDING FINDS

This chapter is given over to the results of much dedicated hard work by a number of colleagues. Do not think for one minute that finds of this quality are the result of good luck: the friends who have given me the opportunity to show these fabulous items have more than 200 years of dedicated detecting experience between them.

What these finds show is that, if you take up the hobby after reading this book and follow the advice given throughout, the opportunity definitely exists for comparable finds to come your

*An impressive haul of silver jewellery, together weighing about 1kg.*

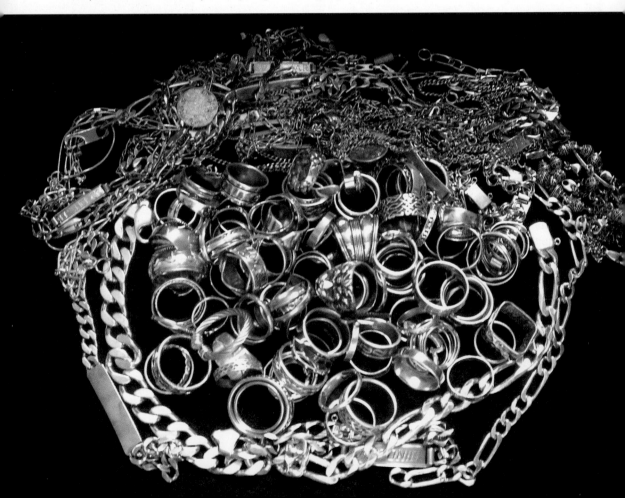

*This heavy 26.9 gram platinum ring was found in shallow water right at the edge of a lagoon.*

way. I have just been told of what could be a truly significant find by a metal detector in northern England. The word is that a hoard of more than 800 Celtic gold stater coins has been discovered, each of which could be valued at around £800. The possible total could be as much as £640,000. Just how must the detectorist and the landowner be feeling? Which one of us is going to beat that?

I will start by showing some of the better pieces of jewellery we have found and then move on to a range of historic finds found by other detectorists of my acquaintance. Some will be quite small individual items and others will be collections built up over many years.

The dream of most detectorists is to find or be part of a group that finds a hoard. The closest I have ever come to finding one was when I was able to assist another member who uncovered a hoard on a club site. The definition of a hoard is when related items or artefacts are found in close proximity and are usually considered to have been hidden or buried with the intention

that they should be recovered at a later date. While the public image of a hoard would probably be a pot full of gold coins, a hoard can consist of coins, jewellery, tools or mixed artefacts.

## MODERN JEWELLERY FINDS

The large platinum ring inset with three diamonds shown in the accompanying photograph as weighing in at an impressive 27 grams, giving it a scrap value at the time of writing of more than £690, was found in about 10cm of water at the very edge of a lagoon. This confirms my earlier advice (see Chapter 14) that when searching in the water it is important to detect right up to the very edge of the beach. Many of my best finds have come from underwater.

Two resplendent jewelled pieces in my collection are of particular interest since they are related to one another. The pendant and ring shown overleaf were found three years and 500km apart in Spain. Coincidently they were

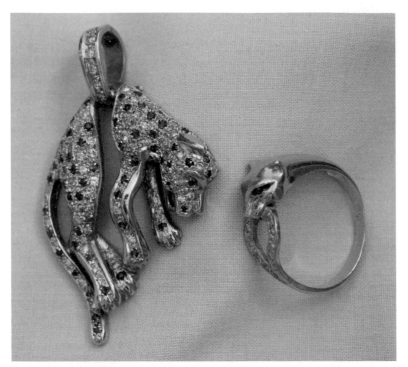

*A 'Cartier' leopard pendant and ring, valued together at nearly £3,500.*

*A stunning 5 carat ruby ring found in France.*

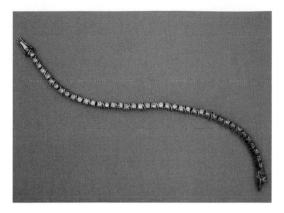

*White gold and topaz bracelet.*

*Large silver and sapphire ring.*

both found in storm gullies about 1.5m below the normal beach level (see Chapter 12). They are copies, rather than fakes, and are inspired by a collection of Cartier panther or leopard pieces designed and made for the Duchess of Windsor by Jeanne Toussaint during the 1940s. These copies are typically produced in the Gold Souk in Dubai; the pendant, which contains 45 grams of 18ct gold and is set with diamonds and sapphires, is valued at £2,880, and the similarly constructed ring is valued at £460.

My wife was responsible for finding the stunning ruby ring opposite on the same bridle path near Béziers that produced the 1576 double sol parisis of Henri III discussed in Chapter 8. It is 18ct gold and dated 1932, and I am advised the ruby weighs 5 carats.

*Unfortunately not every Rolex Oyster watch that's found is genuine; this one's a fake.*

*Silver orb pendant.*

A most unusual find I came across underwater in Spain is a silver pendant that opens out to form a cross. When closed it represents an orb, with no indication that it opens. By pulling on a hidden point with a fingernail, however, the orb rolls out to form a cross made up of pyramidal sections, each of which is engraved on its four sides. Its real beauty, though, is in the intricate engineering that has gone into it. I used to think it was a sort of concealed crucifix, but I have recently been led to believe it might be a fob or pendant used by the Masonic Order. I doubt whether it is particularly valuable, but it is a notable display piece and always of interest to audiences.

## HISTORIC FINDS

The collection of items and displays illustrated here have been found by detectorists in various regions of the country. Their finds may not necessarily have a high monetary value, but all are of historical value and prized by them for that reason.

All of the detectorists had full permission to search from the appropriate landowner and followed the approved codes of conduct as recommended in publications available from the Finds Liaison Officer via your local museum (*see* Chapter 10).

*The orb opens out into an engraved cross.*

*Some of these keys are hundreds of years old. (Martin Brendell)*

Roman bronze statuette of a raven, dating from the second century BC. Ravens were associated with prophecy. (Brian Cavill)

A superb George III gold half guinea of 1803 found on a club site. (Doug Kirk)

Two large Roman brooches: (above) dolphin brooch, 5cm long; (below) crossbow brooch, 6cm long. (Brian Cavill)

# TWO IMPORTANT CASE STUDIES

Either by coincidence or through extraordinary diligence, two of the most significant historic finds made within the general area of North Wiltshire in recent years were made by the same detectorist, Pete Hyams, the first of them being with his 'buddy' Ken James. The two accounts that follow both draw upon his reports of the finds and his memories of the protracted course of events until they were installed in Swindon Museum.

### Wyvern/Wanborough Hoard

The first of these spectacular finds concerns a hoard of Roman coins found by Pete Hyams and Ken James on 31 May 2000 on a site that had been arranged for the use of the Wyvern Historical and Detector Society (WHDS).

Club searches normally take place on a Sunday, but since the field had just been seeded it was decided to hold a search that evening. Pete Hyams was a relative newcomer to the hobby but Ken James was an experienced detectorist. After about half an hour Pete picked up a signal that he recognized as probably being silver. He recovered the item, cleaned off the soil and identified it as a denarius. Soon another denarius turned, followed by more. Following club rules, he called over Dave Ebbage, the club's site officer. By the time he arrived the total had reached ten. Soon everyone joined in the search and coins were being found over an area of ploughed topsoil 10m in diameter. Dave informed the landowner and asked permission to dig down to retrieve the deeper signals concentrated in a patch 2m square in the centre. This main area was then roped off.

As Ken, Dave and Pete started to remove the soil in layers, Pete took photographs of each stage, making sure to include an object of known scale in each photograph. There was no sign of a container; the deepest coin recovered was at 30cm. The whole process took about three hours.

At home Pete carefully washed the coins individually in warm distilled water. He then scanned both sides of all the coins into his computer to provide an accurate record of the find and their condition. The hoard contained a total of 161 denarii, all dated to the reigns of emperors from ad 68 through to ad 180. The emperors represented included Vespasian, Domitian, Nerva, Trajan, Hadrian, Antoninus Pius and Marcus Aurelius. An unusual inclusion was Hadrian's adopted successor, Aelius Caesar, who died shortly before his patron.

They returned to the site the following morning to check it thoroughly for any more coins before putting all the soil back in place. The area was then reseeded. That evening Pete presented the collection to the landowner before handing it over to the correct authorities. In compliance with the Treasure Act the Swindon Coroner was informed of the finds after the weekend.

A week later Pete, Ken and Dave handed the hoard of 161 coins over to the then Curator of the Swindon Museum, Isabella Thompson. Pete made sure that he was given his 'Treasure Receipt', without which he would have no title to the hoard.

Not long after the Coroner, convened the inquest, which was attended by the finders, the landowner and a representative from Swindon Museum. The Coroner examined the coins and heard all the evidence, before declaring that the coins were Treasure. Then, with due correctness, he 'seized the coins on behalf of the Crown' and declared that from then on they would be referred to as the 'Wyvern/Wanborough Hoard'.

The hoard was transferred from the Swindon Museum to the British Museum for cataloguing, cleaning and valuation. After six months the British Museum confirmed that it had no interest in the hoard (denarii are not that rare at national level) and, under the procedure laid out in the Treasure Act, the coins were then offered to other museums in the country.

Swindon Museum indicated that it wished to acquire the hoard. It took nearly two years from the discovery of the hoard to compensation being paid to the landowner and to Pete Hyams, since it took this long for the museum to raise the £4,000 at which the Government Valuation Committee had valued it.

In accordance with the contractual arrangement, this sum was divided equally between the landowner and Pete, who in turn followed the arrangement that many detecting buddies have by splitting his share fifty-fifty with Ken James.

The detector with which Pete found the hoard was a Spectrum Eagle made by White's of Inverness. News of the find was posted on the company's website and Pete received a new White's XLT detector from the company as a reward for all the positive publicity.

### The Saxon Warrior at Wroughton

A few months later, on 11 November 2000, Pete Hyams also discovered the next find – 'why couldn't it be me', said most of the club – on land that he had received permission to detect on following a chance conversation with a friend of the farmer. He was invited to search the land right away, and over the following two years he found artefacts ranging from Roman finds to Victorian

LEFT: *These denarii of Emperor Antoninus Pius (reg AD 138–61), which formed a small part of the hoard, were in superb condition. (Peter Hyams)*

*The view north over the site prior to the excavation. Note the junk on the surface.*

coins. The search map that he made shows a good spread of finds in that particular field and those around.

The field is next to a lay-by and rubbish thrown over the wall led to a large amount of junk showing up in the area but very few finds. Late in the day he started working through the junk, hoping to clear it in case there were some finds beneath. Eventually he heard a more interesting non-ferrous signal. Easing the soil away from the item, it appeared to be a damaged tasting cup or brooch. With time running out he tidied the site, marked the find and went home

Soaking the find in warm distilled water revealed that, although the 'brooch' had suffered plough damage, it was made of bronze and partly gilded, and certainly a significant find of considerable beauty.

The following morning he returned to the site, found the marker and commenced a search, starting with a gridiron pattern on an area of 5m square. Further junk was removed from the site but there were no more significant finds. He

*A damaged Saxon brooch. (D. Philpotts)*

**Key**

| Symbol | Description | Symbol | Description |
|---|---|---|---|
| ● (grey) | Saxon burial site | ✕ | Coins under 300 years of age |
| ▲ | Hammered Elizabethan coin | ● | Roman coins |
| ➤ | Crotal bell | ■ | Roman artefacts |
| ◉ | Hodeen ring | ✳ | Cnut penny |
| ◖ | Dandy ring | ● (light grey) | Pewter buttons |

*Map of the field where the Saxon warrior was buried, showing the spread of finds. (Peter Hyams)*

then started a double gridiron search pattern (see Chapter 4) and on this second search the detector indicated a good solid signal. He dug around the area of the signal before raking the soil away by hand, using a pinpoint detector to locate the target. There in the hole was the undamaged twin of the brooch he had already found, in original condition and of Saxon style.

Nearby there were some small bones that possibly appeared to be human. Following the correct procedure, as it is illegal to remove anything from a gravesite, he informed the farmer of the finds and the rules concerning discoveries of this possible importance, particularly if a body could be buried there. Pete was just in time, since the following morning the field was scheduled to be deep ploughed, which would have destroyed the site. His only option was to rope off the area around the finds and stay there until the tractor had finished ploughing.

The next day he took the brooches and bones to the Swindon Museum. They advised him to report the discovery to the police. After a few days the police reported that the forensic department considered the bones to be from animals and were of no interest. Unwilling to let things go, he decided to contact Wiltshire Archaeology so that they could look more closely at the site.

*Another Saxon brooch after careful restoration. (D. Philpotts and Pete Hyams)*

Bernard Phillips, a respected local independent archaeologist, undertook an emergency excavation of the site with the permission of the landowner. His official report (reproduced in full, with his kind permission, in Appendix One) is both clear and concise.

The then County Archaeologist for Wiltshire, Roy Canham, described the find as significant and exciting, and complimented Pete on the responsible way in which he had acted and told the museum and archaeologists about the find so quickly.

Excavation revealed two bodies. Many friends and detectorists visited the site to observe the work and help where they could. When the sword was ready to be lifted from the grave, Bernard Phillips turned to Pete and said, 'Peter, I think you should have the honour of lifting the sword'.

As he nervously took hold of the sword's hilt in order to lift it, Pete experienced a curious feeling. Gently trying to ease up the sword, he found that some of the leather scabbard material near the tip of the blade was not totally free and the

*The warrior's sword, photographed early in 2009 before being placed in the exciting 'virtual museum' being created at Swindon Museum. (Swindon Museum and Art Gallery)*

spear

sword

shield

blade flexed, as though the warrior was holding on to his sword.

The artefacts removed from the grave were donated to Swindon Museum where they are on display, although you should check with the museum before you plan a visit as the displays are changed periodically.

The whole episode is a fine example of how all the interested parties can work together in a correct and constructive manner towards a successful outcome. It brings together many of the themes discussed throughout this book:

- If Peter had not asked the friend of the farmer he would not have had the introduction to him.
- If his presentation to the farmer had been poor, the farmer may not have given him permission.
- If he had not been systematic and positive, and decided to detect the lay-by area and clear the junk, there would be no find.

- If he had not persevered and gone back there would be no second brooch and bones.
- If he had not returned and guarded the site from ploughing, the site would have been destroyed.
- If he had not followed his instincts and questioned the outcome of the police investigation there would have been no find.
- If he had not sought professional help, there would have been no archaeological investigation.
- If Peter and the farmer had not worked responsibly in partnership with the local community and donated the finds from the grave to Swindon Museum, there would be no display for the public to view.

**Remember, Good Luck is spelt H. A. R. D. W. O. R. K.**

OPPOSITE: *The grave of the Saxon warrior during excavation. The sword, shield and spears are clearly visible. The photo was taken immediately before the sword was lifted. This find was of a pagan burial; later Christian burials would not have included any artefacts and therefore may not have been located by the metal detector. (Peter Hyams)*

# THE BERNARD PHILLIPS REPORT

### A Preliminary Report on the Sixth Century Saxon Burial Site at Brimble Hill, Wroughton

### 25th to 27th September 2000
### by Bernard Phillips

## Introduction

The author was approached by Mr. Peter Hyams, a metal detector user, to investigate the site of archaeological remains he had located in a ploughed field at Brimble Hill, Wroughton. The finds comprised of a pair of large gilded Saxon saucer brooches and bones. Taken to Swindon Museum the bones were identified as probably human and he was advised to show them to the police. This he did, but they identified them as animal. Following agreement, and with permission of the farmer, the author aided by Peter Hyams and others opened a trench 2.0 metres by 2.5 metres around the spot from which the finds had come. Metal detector signals had also indicated at this point the presence of further metal artefacts.

## The Site

At 165 metres O.D., the site of the discovery lies on the edge of the chalk escarpment that rises from the Kimmeridge clay plateau that surrounds Swindon Hill. The latter is a prominent feature in the wide ranging views from the ridge. The field, owned by Mr Nick Gosling of Wood Farm, Wroughton, has been cultivated for many years.

**The Excavation**

Removal of the top soil revealed at a depth of 19 cms a packed chalk surface levelled by ploughing. In it the outline of a linear feature could be defined. At the north end of this feature two holes dug by Peter Hyams could be seen. Removal of their fill revealed in the side of the northern most a damaged amber bead. From this hole had come the saucer brooches. Iron work exposed at the bottom of the other lay at a greater depth.

Removal of a layer of large chalk blocks, exposed two human skeletal remains. One poorly preserved, evidently a child, partly overlay the infilling of the other's grave pit.

The child's grave measured 48 cms wide, 1.60 metres long. Its depth below the plough soil varied from 9 to 11 cms. The lower fill of the grave comprised of a silty loam mixed with chalk blocks. Aligned 22° west of magnetic north the child had been laid extended on its back, head to the south, with legs crossed and the left lower arm bent across the stomach. It would appear, from their location, that the two saucer brooches and the amber bead had come from the foot of this grave.

Measuring 1.40 metres by 2.20 metres the lower grave had its base at 16 to 22 cms below the plough soil. The grave's lower fill comprised of chalk blocks mixed with a silty loam.

Within the grave the decayed skeletal remains of an adult male lay, aligned 30° west of magnetic north, on his right side with his legs drawn up. His head lay to the south. Originally it had been placed face up, but over time the jaw had dropped and the skull had rolled onto its top. Cradled in his right arm lay an iron sword. East of the sword hilt, two iron spearheads lay together. They had been laid so that their shafts crossed the burials thighs. Located between the sword and the skeleton's pelvis lay a shield's domed central boss, it was this that the metal detector had registered. Two iron studs were found adjacent to each other on opposing sides of the boss. Most likely they had fixed the shield's hand grip in place and provided decoration on the shield's exterior. Two of the studs lay on top of the sword blade showing that the shield had been placed over the man's upper body after positioning of the sword and presumably the spears. Beneath the sword, near to its tip, a small iron buckle was uncovered. It is probable that this came from the shoulder strap that would have held the sword.

### The Skeletons

Both skeletons have been left in the ground.

The child's skeleton had badly decayed due to the acidic nature of the bedrock and grave fill. Surviving bones comprised of the cranium, some loose teeth, both upper arms (humerus), part of the lower left arm (ulna and radius), the pelvis, both thigh bones (femur) and half of the left leg (tibia and fibula). The height of the child was around 1.16 metres (3 feet 9½ inches). Its age would therefore be around five or six years. The presence of the amber bead and a pair of brooches make it likely that the child was female.

The adult skeleton is better preserved although the bones are fragile. On the skull the facial area had been badly crushed, but the upper jaw (maxilla) and the upper part of the left eye socket, having a prominent brow ridge, were recognisable. The lower jaw (mandible) had all its teeth present as would appear the upper jaw. Much of the spine had decayed although several neck vertebrae survived intact. Many of the ribs existed as did all the arm bones (humerus, ulna and radius). Some hand bones (metacarpus and metacarpul) remained, those on the body's right side lay on the right thigh (femur). Both legs survived (femur, patella, tibia and fibula) as did most of the bones of the right foot (talus, naricula, metatarsul and phalanx). Only a few bones (metatarsul) of the left foot were found.

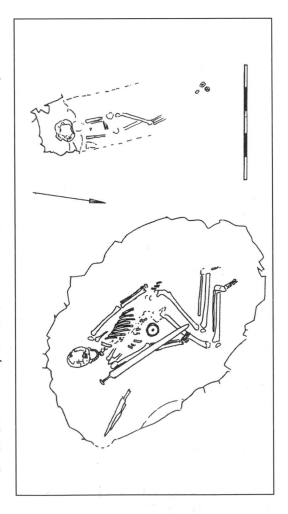

Using the equation determined by Trotter and Gelser (1952, 1958) the tibia measurements give the skeleton's height as having been 180 cms (5 feet 11 inches). Fairly excessive attrition on the lower mandible's molars when compared to the chart in 'Digging Up

*The Brimble Hill Saxon burials.*

Bones' (Brothwell, 1965) suggests that he died between thirty-five and forty-five years of age. No trauma to the limbs or skull was evident. The appearance of the bones suggest that the person had a slender build.

## The Finds

### Child's Grave
Three artefacts were recovered from the foot of the grave, evidently placed there, perhaps in a container or on clothing.

### Saucer brooches
The two large cast bronze saucer brooches, approximately 8 cms diameter, are in the possession of Peter Hyams and have not been presented for examination. They were briefly viewed by the author. Both are identical although one has suffered damage, most likely from a strike by a plough-share. Internally the surface is gilded. The decoration of a 'chip-carving' technique commences at the outer edge of the saucer's base below a wide rim. At the centre a small cross lies within a circle, around this is a ring of inward pointing bars, two long, two short and two long repeated four times. Enclosing this are a further five concentric rings. The second and third of these, from the outside, are interrupted at four equally spaced positions by single inward pointing V-shapes. Traces of an iron pin with a bronze catch plate and pin attachment plate survive on the brooches' rear.

The brooches would have been worn one at each shoulder to hold a cloak in place. Pairs are often found in female graves whilst men usually have one.

Saucer brooches can be of fifth or sixth century date, but the large size of these would suggest the later period.

### Amber bead
The damaged bead of irregular shape measures 1.9 cms long and 1.7 cms by originally 1.9 cms across. It is pierced by a small hole for suspension from a cord.

Amber was thought to have prophylactic virtues and so had a defence against witchcraft. This yellowish fossil resin comes from extinct pine forests and is found washed onto the shores of the Baltic and the coast of East Anglia. The Baltic trade via the Danube dates back to prehistoric times, but a short lived trade in Anglia amber apparently occurred in the second half of the sixth century.

## Adult's Grave
Carefully positioned in the grave the nine iron items recovered are the trappings of a warrior.

## The sword
Well preserved, the iron sword has a blade length of 78.5 cms and at its widest measures 5 cms across. The blade's thickness varies from 0.62 cms near the hilt to 0.36 cms near the point. The tang is 10.5 cms long and tapers from 1.1 cms to 2.1 cms, and has a thickness of 0.73 cms. Attached to the tang a pommel measures 4.6 cms long, 0.8 cms at its widest and 0.91 cms thick. Amongst the corrosive products on the rear of the sword, as uncovered, traces of the leather scabbard remain. The leather covers about 10% of the surface and includes the sheath's top edge. Traces of a wooden hilt also survives.

## The sheath's shoulder strap buckle
This small iron buckle of D-shape measures 2.4 cms long, 1.5 cms wide and 0.5 cms thick.

## The shield boss
With a flange 1.3 cms wide the well-preserved iron shield boss has an overall diameter of 12.6 cms. The central dome has a height of 6.9 cms. Central to the top a bronze? stud stands a further 0.8 cms high. Its flat upper surface 1.0 cms in diameter is gilded. On the underside of the flange that is 0.3 cms thick, traces of five iron stud shafts are discernible, their positions suggests a further three exists. Also adhering to the flange are traces of the wooden construction of the shield.

## The handle attachment studs
These four identical circular topped iron studs measure 2.2 cms in diameter. Their upper surface is slightly domed and they vary in thickness from 0.24 cms to 0.31 cms. Part of the shaft, 0.54 cms square, survives on two of the studs One stud also has traces of wood or leather adhering.

## The long spearhead (stabbing?)
Measuring 45.1 cms overall the large spearhead has a socket 10.4 cms long and 2.3 cms in

diameter at the mouth. The blade 2.9 cms at its widest has a thickness which tapers from 0.92 cms near the socket to 0.37 cms near the point.

**The short spearhead (throwing?)**
The socket of the small spearhead measures 9.0 cms long and has a diameter of 2.3 cms at the mouth. At its widest point the blade measures 2.9 cms and its length is 15.2 cms. The thickness of the blade tapers from 0.67 cms near the socket to 0.37 cms near the point.

## Conclusions

The discovery, at Brimble Hill, of two Saxon burials strongly suggests that this is the site of a cemetery. The fact that one grave cut the other indicates that burials took place here over a long period of time.

Following the discovery a search by metal detector around the grave site recorded over a wide area the presence of a lot of iron. Normally metal detectors are programmed to ignore iron, evidencing why despite years of searching no burials had previously been encountered in the field.

Cemetery sites have previously been recorded on the top edge of the chalk escarpment at Bassett Down House, found during landscaping and Foxhill near Wanborough found in cutting a pipe trench. Both cemeteries were nor properly excavated. A single burial was also discovered at the cross road just above Wanborough by workmen.

# APPENDIX TWO

# THE SOCIETY OF THAMES MUDLARKS AND ANTIQUARIANS

*Sebastian Melmo*

The Mudlarks is a name popularized by Henry Mayhew in his writings on the London Underworld in the 1860s. His is a tale of desperately poor children beyond the boundaries of the harshly divisive Victorian economy. They were frequently homeless children who survived by combing the Thames foreshore at low tides for anything they could sell on, such as coal, wood, copper, fat, iron and canvas. They survived on their wits and ingenuity against constant and often deserved harassment from authority, for they were always open to opportunistic stealing from the many barges and boats that used the river. Just over a hundred years after Mayhew was recording the activities of London's low life a very different type of Mudlark began to appear on the beaches of the Thames.

Towards the end of the 1970s the growing number of independent enthusiasts searching the Thames foreshore at low water began to experience a variety of challenges from the authorities in respect to their activities. The individuals concerned came from a mixture of backgrounds but all had a passion for searching the mud for the many fascinating and informative objects left behind along the way of London's long history.

Their activities ranged from surface searching by eye to the use of some of the most sophisticated metal detectors of the time. Controversy arose as searchers became ever more energetic in actually digging holes in their search for more and earlier finds. It gradually became apparent that recovery of all manner of well-preserved artefacts from almost two thousand years of activity was possible. The prospect was good with productive docks, barge beds and beaches along both banks of the Thames throughout its length in the City of London and beyond. At first activities were conducted without control, coordination or recording of finds. Digging holes on the foreshore was, of course, both illegal and dangerous. The Metropolitan Police became ever more vigilant in chasing people off the mud. Although the Museum of London seemed to give scant regard to the potential of excavating the riverfront, they too became alarmed at the potential loss of important artefacts.

For those whose hobby was working the foreshore, searching became more difficult as none of the parties involved really seemed to understand the implications of what was developing. The situation worsened and it began to look as if it would be impossible to continue searching without being in trouble with the law. Covert attempts were made to search and dig at night or to detect hidden from view under bridges or covered foreshore, such as the old Customs House quays by Billingsgate. As pressure on searchers increased, cooperation developed between them. They joined forces and formed themselves into The Society of Thames Mudlarks and Antiquarians, thus establishing a coordinated and reasonable force to challenge the authorities. Some thirty individuals elected an honorary president and committee and began to hold regular meetings formulating a campaign to be allowed to continue their activities.

Meetings were held with the Port of London Authority, the Metropolitan Police and the Museum of London. A long struggle ensued to maintain the hobby as a viable activity. By the early 1980s agreements were more or less reached and a set of rules and regulations were written down and permits issued upon a modest payment to the Port of London Authority. Certain designated areas such as national monuments were to be out of bounds, all finds were to be reported to the Museum of London and holes were to be completely filled in before being covered by the next tide. Membership was limited to sixty individuals, new members having to prove their integrity to the new code of practice during a probationary period. The Society became affiliated to the Federation of Independent Detectorists (FID) and members were covered by substantial public liability insurance. Regular meetings were held in the function rooms of famous riverside pubs. The George at Southwark eventually became the regular venue and guest speakers, professional archaeologists and amateurs were invited to give talks on their specialist subjects, their collections or technical data on metal detectors or collection housing.

It was, however, a rocky course with continual intervention by the authorities. Not always without good reason, there were mavericks that chose to stay outside the control of the Society and indeed members within the Society that found it impossible to abide by simple regulation. This led to some abusive reporting in the press and a strong anti-lobby among professional archaeologists. From the academic point of view there was the loss, indeed loss without record, of cultural material filtering into obscurity via the markets without documentation or provenance attached. They had a point and it is undoubtedly to history's loss that the Museum of London did not earlier develop a strong rescue plan for the river shore or have a more proactive and less apathetic acquisitions policy regarding finds taken from the river by amateurs.

Much of the professional disinterest in river finds emanated from the archaeologists' view that there was no detectable stratification descending through the foreshore and so little historic value could be attached to the objects retrieved. However, for those now experienced in digging and detecting the foreshore and confronted by literally many thousands of objects spanning two centuries and beyond, it became very easy to identify and date almost everything that was found. Most of those working the foreshore became highly proficient at arranging the subjects of their interests into a chronological order or type or region of manufacture. The wealth of material coming up and the huge corporate historical knowledge of the membership had produced a panel of experts. Society members became specialist in periods and types of artefact, coins, pottery, tools, spoons, keys, clay pipes, ships fittings and so on.

A practised eye was kept for unusual bones or geological peculiarities. Substantial specialist collections were built up, provenance was

*The silt has helped keep these carpenters' tools in perfect preservation. (Martin Brendell)*

persisted through the continual criticism that was levelled against them from some quarters.

Issues of safety were addressed seriously by the Society. The membership was kept informed of dangers such as Weil's decease (Leptospirosis), a potentially fatal disease contracted from water contaminated with rat urine. The dangers of deep hole digging, mud slip and burial were high on the safety agenda, as was the correct course of action to be taken when unexploded bombs were located. Probably the most controversial subject relating to safety was the vital need to fill in holes before they were overcome by the tide and filled with water. The danger was considerable, as the murky waters of the river gave no hint that a deep hole was anything other than a shallow puddle come next low tide.

Those that would not comply with the safety needs of 'filling in' were expelled from the Society after a warning. The authorities would not issue a permit to non-Mudlarks and so the penalty of exclusion hung over offenders who then found themselves outside the law if they continued to operate on the river.

Always attendant on riverbank digging is the troublesome subject of erosion and this was certainly a concern of the authorities in granting permits to dig the Thames foreshore. This, and a concern for surface and sub-surface wildlife, did eventually lead to a drastic reduction in permitted digging depths. These justifiable concerns were acted upon very late in the day and although they are now stringently applied they came after the great tide of amateur discovery over two decades. There was undoubtedly some erosion as a result of the intensity of digging and loosening of sub-layers in some areas but without any great loss of structure. Some Victorian barge-beds and their revetments disappeared; however, no permanent structures of any historical importance

recorded and some important and erudite publications were produced in cooperation with the professional archaeologists at the Museum of London. It is to the great credit of these archaeologists that they sought to tap the fount of finds and knowledge offered by the Mudlarks' activities that these important studies reached print in the appropriate journals. It is also to the credit of the Mudlarks' membership that so much enthusiasm to communicate their finds to authority were uncovered other than the burnt stumps of jetties destroyed in the Great Fire.

There was, of course, the thrill of treasure hunting; the subject of fortunes to be made was ever a camp follower of the Mudlarks. It is true that some dug 'professionally' and there was certainly a great deal of money made by some members of the Society selling finds on the antiquities market. The Museum of London was shown most of the material excavated by the Mudlarks over their years of activity and were duly given the opportunity to purchase items before or if they were ever offered on a broader market. Indeed on more than one occasion sums in excess of £20,000 were raised for items of special interest. The Museum was not held to ransom as some have suggested at times. On the contrary members of the Society were keen to see items of interest go into the permanent collections of the Museum. Much was presented with pride over the years and it is highly likely that further material will be acquired by bequest in the future. Sadly had the Museum developed a better collections development policy and sharpened its fund-raising abilities, much more would certainly have been saved for study and future reference.

Metal detectors were undoubtedly the 'machine' that made this rapid discovery and exploitation of the River's treasure by amateurs possible. Organized excavation, other than possibly the expensive process of coffer damming some of the more important docks such as Queenhithe, probably never was an option. Metalwork including ferrous objects was almost always perfectly preserved in the anaerobic conditions of the river silt, which was compacted to a near dry condition over the centuries.

*The maker's marks are still visible on a pair of beautifully restored padlocks. (Martin Brendell)*

This made digging on the Thames a unique experience for those lucky enough to have been part of it. Traditionally professional archaeologists have been passionately outspoken against metal detectors. This quite justifiably stems mainly from the numerous damaging reports of vandalism and theft by rogue detectorists invading heritage sites and National Monuments.

An interesting reversal of this usual sad story was the cooperation that developed between the Mudlarks and archaeologists engaged in rescue digs along the developing Thames waterfront. Behind the present waterfront are buried revetments, lanes, building foundations, yards and foreshores covered by the successive infilling and narrowing of the river as the City enlarged ever further onto newly claimed ground. At times of boom building, and now with excavation of foundations to prehistoric levels, outrageously little time is afforded the archaeologists in their last chance to record great swathes of London's past.

During recent times of pressure the Museum of London accepted the volunteer help of the membership of The Society of Thames Mudlarks, who frequently worked a supervised rota of metal detecting on the threatened sites. Consequently many thousands of potentially lost items were retrieved for the respective rescue dig reports. So impressive were the efforts of the volunteers that the archaeologists finally took on board the effectiveness of metal detectors and began using them 'officially' under the initial tuition of the Thames Mudlarks.

Of the finds themselves, just about every artefact that might come to mind has been found. Coins, of course, and occasionally even a coin die. The many small personal objects found included rings, buckles, pins, belt chapes, purse frames, buttons and simple toys etc, and all became targets for specialist collections. Iron tools, horseshoes, fishhooks, padlocks, keys, knives and even edged weapons were found in superb condition because of the oxygen-free environment they were taken from. Arrowheads and fragments of chain mail were always exciting to find. Occasionally chain mail links bore tiny makers marks. Pewter also survived well and competition ran high to find the little medieval pilgrim badges thrown into the river by devotees returning from shrines all over Europe. Clay pipes, glass and pottery suffered in hasty digging, as they were non-detectable, however, many complete items were recovered such as small fourteenth-century pitchers, bellarmine bottles and later tin-glazed ointment pots. A continuing list here would not do justice to the huge spectrum of exciting recoveries. Suffice it to say that the rejectamenta and lost items of London's past have been recovered in huge numbers and in great variety, adding hugely to the documentation of this unique city's past.

Identification of finds has been greatly aided by reference to the Mudlarks' Bible, the *Medieval Catalogue* of the London Museum (later the Museum of London) first published by His Majesty's Stationary Office in 1940 and reprinted many times since. Also, lately published by The Stationary Office, there is the superb series of specialist subject volumes *Medieval Finds from Excavations in London*. The Museum of London itself has, of course, been ever helpful in identification work and their advice has been highly valued by the membership of The Mudlarks. The members themselves have a wealth of self-taught knowledge and active discussion on finds at meetings and after digging mornings around a pub table has been part of the huge enjoyment experienced by those that have been lucky enough to take part. On these later occasions enjoyment of picking over the morning's finds was often shared by amazed onlookers

*A piece of chain mail recovered from the Thames foreshore. (Martin Brendell)*

watching some very muddy people emptying equally muddy debris from a plastic bucket onto a pub table as members identified and swapped items of interest among themselves. It has to be said that there was a delightful Fagin's Den atmosphere about these occasions.

Despite the many setbacks and disappointments suffered by The Society of Thames Mudlarks and Antiquarians, it still thrives as a significant society with a healthy membership regularly surface searching under ever more stringent restrictions. The days of deep digging may be over but the tides regularly offer prizes to those that walk the foreshore with a membership card in their pocket.

# AN INTRODUCTION TO EYES-ONLY SEARCHING

*Darwin Turner*

A wide ranges of artefacts can be seen when out searching and you may wish to start collecting some of them. These notes are intended help you identify and possibly date them. The most common finds are pieces of pottery (shards). You can also expect to find such material as flint, stone, glass, fossils and possibly organic matter, depending on where you are searching.

*Typical items found while field walking.*

## POTTERY

This brief introduction is intended to help the reader approximately date or identify most of the pottery they are likely to find while field walking or metal detecting.

### Should I Collect Pottery?

The first thing you need to decide is whether to pick it up in the first place. If the answer is yes, you need to ask yourself whether you have a place to store it or a satisfactory way of disposing of it when you have finished with it.

Don't be lulled into a false sense of security because you have been searching for a while and not found any pottery. There is a mountain of it out there and you could very well end up with a large part of it under your bed or on top of the wardrobe in cardboard boxes. You might ignore my advice, but you have been warned!

If you choose to go ahead I would suggest that in the first instance you collect all the pot you see and sort through it later. A single shard of pot does not necessarily date a site. Collect all you can and make sense of as large a collection

*Assorted shards of Roman pottery. (Brian Cavill)*

as possible. The collection should give an accurate indication of the dates over which the site was occupied.

### Diagnostic Shards ('Shapes')

Certain parts of pottery shapes are helpful in identifying the overall shape and type of vessel, as well as the date. Rims are the portion where the top of the pot ends. Base shards and the portion of the pot where the side meets the base are most helpful when it comes to dating. Handles and shards showing decoration are also of great value in establishing pottery types.

*Rim Shards*
Rim shards have been looked at for dating purposes for as long as archaeologists have been seriously studying pottery. Look at the material in your local museums or in publications to pick up on local variations.

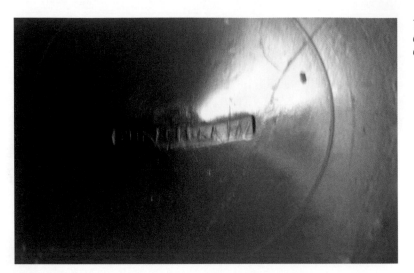

*The Roman potter's mark can be seen quite clearly on this piece. (Brian Cavill)*

*Base Shards*

The following comments provide a simple guide to dating:

- Marks on the bottom of some small Roman pots indicate that they were cut off the wheel while it was still turning.
- Sagging bases indicate a medieval date.
- Bases thumbed down in whole or in part indicate a medieval or post-medieval date.
- Applied feet suggest a post-mediaeval feature.

*Handles*

Traditionally in the medieval and post-medieval period handles were pulled, that is they were made from a lump of clay held in one hand while being shaped and pulled with the other hand.

Some Roman pottery followed an altogether different tradition with their handles being thrown; this gives such handles similar sections to those on the rim of the pot. The same happens with mediaeval imports from Europe.

*Decoration*

Applied decoration is often called sprigging; I would think of it as probably medieval but would look at the other indicators as well.

Faces on pots, either applied or just moulded or cut, can be Roman as well as a medieval feature. Geometric patterns or scenes of people or animals are normally Roman in date.

Pots decorated by pressing the wet clay into a mould to form the pot are likely to be Roman.

*Stamped Marked Pieces*

If you are lucky you might find a bit with a maker's name on it. Makers' marking their wares was popular in the Roman period and is useful in dating material. Makers' marks are well documented and are accurate indicators of date as they changed rapidly over time.

The practice of makers marking their wares did not reappear until the Industrial Revolution when it became commonplace again.

The Romans used pottery plates; such wares did not come back into fashion until the post-mediaeval period. That does not mean plates did not exist, just that instead of pottery they were metal or wood.

## Dating

The popularly accepted dates for the various periods in history are:

| Neolithic | 2700 BC – 1900 BC |
| Bronze Age | 1900 BC – 500 BC |
| Iron Age | 500 BC – 55/54 BC or AD 43 |
| Roman | 55/54 BC or AD 43 – AD 410 |
| Saxon | AD 410 – 1066 |
| Medieval | 1066 – 1485 |
| Post-Medieval | 1485 – 1837 |
| Modern | 1837 – present |

Start and end dates of any particular period may vary depending on who is writing and their point of view, or their reading of such things as radiocarbon dating and tree ring analysis.

The form of the clay used, known as the fabric, is invaluable for quick estimates of dating. Look at the material through a hand lens or magnifying glass. If you take a nineteenth-century hand-thrown flowerpot as your example, you will better understand what I mean. The grain size of the bits in a pottery shard (a broken piece of pottery) will tell you a lot about the date of the pot.

As a general rule, pottery before the late Iron Age was very coarse. During the Roman period the body (the material the pot was made from) became finer, almost as fine as our nineteenth-century flowerpot.

Saxon pottery becomes very coarse again, with the very earliest having organic temper (material deliberately added to the wet clay) to aid with the firing. Middle and late Saxon pottery is coarse with shell temper.

Medieval pottery gets less coarse as time passes. As we enter the post-medieval period (from 1485) clay bodies are as fine as our flowerpot example.

With the discovery of china clay and ball clay in Cornwall during the seventeenth century clay bodies became finer and finer, also whiter and whiter. This was due in the main to the ease of transport of raw materials between Cornwall and Stoke-on-Trent and the rising demand from consumers for white china utensils. The whiteness we see today was already achieved by the 1770s. Changes in glaze, shape and decoration are key indicators of date between the late eighteenth century and the present.

## Glazes

The Romans did make glazed pottery, but it was of high status and is not common.

The regular use of glazing starts in the medieval period. At first only part of the pot was glazed. As time passed more and more of the surface of the pot was glazed, until we arrive at the present day when pots are glazed all over, inside and out.

## Earthenware, Stoneware or Porcelain?

Earthenware is not vitrified (with all the particles glued together by heat) and will draw on your tongue when you place the broken edge of the shard on it tongue; try this on your flowerpot and see what I mean. Some will draw more than others, but it is an indication. You will find earthenware at all dates.

Stoneware is vitrified and won't draw your tongue. It can be grey (most commonly) or red. The external glaze on salt-glazed stoneware is applied by throwing salt into the kiln during the heating cycle and the chemical action forms the glaze. The surface is described as looking like orange peel.

Porcelain again is vitrified, so it won't draw your tongue. It has an applied glaze that can be seen when viewed through a hand lens. Most of the porcelain you will find is of eighteenth- and nineteenth-century date. If it has any other colour than blue assume a later rather than an earlier date. If the blue is not clear blue you might have a piece of pre-eighteenth-century date. This would indicate high status.

### What Shape Pot Does My Shard Come From?

Pots that are thrown on a wheel have lines inside and out where the potter's fingers and tools have left telltale lines. If you hold up the shard and look along the lines so that they appear horizontal you can get an impression of the shape of the pot. Pots also tend to thin towards the top, although this isn't always the case.

## BUILDING MATERIALS

### Roof Tiles

Roof tiles were used extensively in the Roman period, where high status buildings need roofing and natural stone was not available. Roman tile types include the tegula, flat with turned-up edges and about 15 to 20mm thick, and the imbrex, which is curved and a little thinner. Fancy ridge end-pieces called finials were also used and are a clear indication of Roman date and high status.

After the Roman period the manufacture of roof tiles in Britain went out of fashion, even if using them didn't. Roman roof tiles appear as building materials for walls in a significant number of early Saxon buildings.

The manufacture of flat and thinner roof tiles started in the Tudor period and continues today. Flat roof tiles are a tradition in southeast England, while pantiles in the East Anglian tradition were used extensively elsewhere in the country during the nineteenth and twentieth centuries, being transported by the railways.

### Floor Tiles

The Romans were the first to introduce floor tiles. Their large tiles were about 23cm square and about 2.5cm thick. They were used to floor rooms and also build the columns (*pilae*) that supported the floors of the rooms with under-floor heating.

After the end of the Roman period floor tiles suffered the same fate as the roof tiles and ended up in Saxon buildings.

The medieval period saw the reintroduction of floor tiles.

### Bricks

Bricks appear in the Roman period and look like Roman floor tiles. They also suffered the same fate as other Roman building materials and reappear in Saxon buildings. A typical shape 23cm square and 2.5cm thick would be a good place to start your thinking.

When bricks reappeared in the Tudor period they had morphed into the rectangular form we now recognize as a brick, as opposed to a tile. Tudor bricks were thinner than modern bricks and were also made without a frog (the roof-shaped dimple in the brick).

### Tesserae (Mosaics)

Tesserae are the pieces of ceramic and stone that make up mosaics. High status mosaics were made of small (about 18mm) and very small pieces. Mosaics of a lower status, or laid in low status parts of a high status building, would use tesserae significantly larger than 18mm type. Pottery is used for the smaller tesserae, while building materials were used for the larger pieces. Natural stone was used in all sizes: the distance it had to be transported to the site is a good indication of status, which increased as distance increased.

## MUSEUMS AND ORGANIZATIONS

### Visit Museums

A visit to a local museum will show you instantly the most significant types of pottery found in your area and might answer many questions in one visit. You might need to make enquiries to find a local museum that exhibits pieces of broken pottery, as not all do.

There are several museums around the country with extensive displays of Roman pottery. I have recently visited the National Roman Legion Museum at Carleon in South Wales, but there is an equally good one in Colchester. Roman pottery is well studied and of uniform manufacture, so you should have few problems there.

A visit to the Potteries Museum and Art Gallery in Stoke-on-Trent will show you the products of what was once one of the most important pottery manufacturing centres in the world. In the eighteenth and nineteenth centuries pottery was sent from Stoke-on-Trent all over the British Isles. If your finds were made in Stoke at that time you will be able to see complete examples in their collection.

The Finds Liaison Officer (FLO) in your local museum might or might not be able to tell you what you've found, but there is a support network to which the shard could be sent for identification.

Build your own reference collection. If you keep the material you find in boxes or bags for each site it won't take long before you have a good reference collection enabling you to date your search areas.

### Local Libraries

The local history section in your local or central library will hold the relevant publications; enquire online, by phone or in person. I am a great believer in popping into my local library and just asking. I am sure an obscure query about Saxon or medieval pottery is more interesting than a request for the latest bodice-ripper. Don't be intimidated by librarians; some of my best friends are librarians.

### English Heritage

Make enquires at English Heritage in person and online. I consider myself most fortunate as their head office is in my home town of Swindon. The public can use their library in person, allowing readers to sign in and leave their bags at the front desk. It is the best library I know for finding the material you will need to track down your pottery reports.

*Flint tools and a stone hand axe. (Brian Cavill)*

# AN INTRODUCTION TO FLINT AND STONE

This is the subsection I would rather someone else had been asked to write. The reason is simple: I have lost more friends than I care to remember by telling them that the flint tool that they thought was so special was really only a piece that had been hit by the plough or was wholly natural and caused by frost.

Flint is a form of natural glass and habitually breaks with a conchoidal (shell-like) fracture when struck. It is this predictability that makes flint the first choice for knapping in the British Isles. Knapping is the art or craft of striking off flakes by hitting the flint with a tool such as a stone (hammer stone) or a hammer (iron hammer) of appropriate size.

The core is what remains when you strike off blades/flakes from a piece of flint. A blade is a flake, usually three or four times longer than it is wide.

## Flint-Using Periods

Flint was used in the Palaeolithic (the Old Stone Age) the Mesolithic (the Middle Stone Age) the Neolithic (the New Stone Age) – the age of the first farmers – and the Bronze Age, the time when technology changed and bronze, an alloy of copper and tin, was introduced for some high status artefacts. Throughout the Bronze Age flint remained the material of choice for making things such as arrowheads and scrapers.

## Stone Tools Made of Materials Other than Flint

Hammer stones for making flint tools can be flint, but they are usually some other sort of stone. In Wiltshire I have found quartzite pebbles that had been selected from the Thames gravels for use as hammer stones. In my garden I also found an old flint core that I think was used as a hammer stone.

Hammer stones reflect the size of the work they were used for. Big flakes – big hammer stones. Little flakes – little hammer stones. What you will notice on the hammer stone is the crushing of the end that was used to strike the flint. The shape of people's hands hasn't changed markedly since the Stone Age and once one had a hammer stone that fitted the hand that's the way it would have been used, over and over again. Wear therefore would have occurred in the same place time and time again, leaving the traces of wear that identify the pebble as a tool.

### Querns

With the coming of the Neolithic the quern, a simple grain grinder, appears in the material culture. The original querns were saddle querns that have a fat sausage-shaped stone placed on top of a flat or slightly dished stone. The grinding takes place by crushing the grain as the smaller is moved over the larger.

In evolutionary terms the rotary quern followed on from the saddle quern. The rotary quern has a polo-shaped stone that could be rotated on top of a stationary stone with a hump in it. The shape and position of the hole in the top stone to take the handle changed over time, as did the shape of the stones.

## GLASS

Glass is something you will find from time to time. Ancient glass, with its attractive opalescent surface, is a health hazard and should be treated as such. Health and safety is important and if you intend to collect this material it is essential that you consider an appropriate risk analysis.

The Romans used glass for both windows and containers. It was valuable and recycled, a practice that has reduced the amount available to find on a Roman site. The Romans made free-blown as well as mould-blown glass, so shape in the first instance might not be a good indicator of date. They applied nice handles to some of their bottles and flasks. Since these are both thicker and more durable, as well as of characteristic shape and design, they might make a better bet to be collected

Glass in the Saxon period is very beautiful indeed, usually very thin and extremely fragile.

During the late medieval period glass became more common but it remained a high status item. Glass was made in this country as well as being imported. Local/British glass would indicate a high status site; together with imported glass it would indicate a very high status site.

## FOSSILS

Why should a metal detectorist be interested in fossils as they give no indication of occupation and hence no indication of lost metal finds? I agree and collect them for their own sake. Some detector clubs have an eyes-only section in their 'find of the month' competition and fossils can be entered in this section.

All the artefacts listed above have something in common in that they are all inorganic, not organic material of plant or animal origin that will usually have decomposed over time. In exceptional circumstances this process has been avoided: we know how Mesolithic flints were hafted or shafted, for example, because complete tools have been recovered form sites where the usual decomposition of organic matter has not taken place.

# SIGNALS USING A MINELAB XTERRA 30 DETECTOR

| Item | Number | Signal pitch | Type of signal |
| --- | --- | --- | --- |
| **£2 coin** | 32–36 | High, medium | Alternate clipped |
| **£1 coin** | 28–32 | High, high | Alternate sharp |
| **50p** | 16 | Medium | Soft smooth |
| **20p** | 20 | Medium | Strong smooth |
| **10p** | 18–20 | Medium | Soft smooth |
| **5p** | 18–20 | Medium | Soft smooth |
| **2p** | 36–40 | High | Alternate clipped |
| **1p** | 36 | High | Sharp clipped |
| **Silver paper** | 4 | Medium | Strong rounded |
| **Ring pull** | 16–20 | Medium | Strong clipped |
| **Gold ring** | 9 or 12 | Medium | Double clipped |
| **Silver ring** | 36 | High | Double clipped |
| **Iron** | Minus | Deep | Mushy soft |
| **Lead** | 36–40 | High | Sharp clipped |
| **Aluminium** | 44 | High | Sharp clipped |

# USEFUL CONTACTS

## PERIODICALS

*Treasure Hunting*
The Publishing House
119 Newland Street
Witham
Essex CM8 1WF
Tel: 01376 521900
E-mail: info@treasurehunting.co.uk
www.treasurehunting.co.uk

*The Searcher*
17 Down Road
Merrow
Guildford
Surrey GU1 2PX
Tel: 01483 830133
E-mail: info@thesearcher.co.uk
www.thesearcher.co.uk

Both *Treasure Hunting* and *The Searcher* provide valuable information on news and events, and the advertising carried is a guide to retailers, distributors, hardware and services.

## SPECIALIST BOOKS ON METAL DETECTING

**Greenlight Publishing**
119 Newland Street
Witham
Essex CM8 1WF
Tel: 01376 521900
E-mail: books@greenlightpublishing.co.uk
www.greenlightpublishing.co.uk

## SELECTED MANUFACTURERS

**Minelab International Ltd**
Laragh
Bandon
Co. Cork
Ireland
E-mail: minelab@minelab.ie
www.minelab.com

**White's Electronics (UK) Ltd**
35 Harbour Road
Inverness IV1 1UA
Tel: 01463 223456
E-mail: info@whites.co.uk
wwwwhites.co.uk

## SELECTED DETECTOR SUPPLIERS

### Leisure Promotions
Unit 8
The Kennet Centre
Newbury
Berkshire RG14 5EN
Tel: 01635 46040
E-mail: info@leisure-promotions.co.uk
www.leisure-promotions.co.uk

### Joan Allen Electronics Ltd
190 Main Road
Biggin Hill
Kent TN16 3BB
Tel: 01959 571255
E-mail: sales@joanallen.co.uk
www.joanallen.co.uk

### Regton Ltd
82 Cleveland Street
Birmingham B19 3SN
Tel: 0121 359 2379
E-mail: sales@regton.com
www.regton.com

## SELECTED SUPPLIERS

### H. S. Walsh & Sons Ltd
243 Beckenham Road
Beckenham
Kent BR3 4TS
Tel: 020 8778 7061
Fax: 020 8676 8669
E-mail: mail@hswalsh.com
www.hswalsh.com
Complete jewellery supplies including precious
metals, tools, cleaning and polishing materials.

### Cookson Precious Metals
59–83 Vittoria Street
Birmingham B1 3NZ
Tel: 0121 212 6421
www.cooksonsgold.com
Buyers and sellers of precious metals; tools and
equipment suppliers.

### ABC Polishing and Engineering Supplies
103 Louth Road
Holton Le Clay
Grimsby
Lincolnshire DN36 5AD
Tel: 01472 824520
Formerly Cetem Polishing Supplies. Polishing
supplies and training courses.

### Unifix
Shire Business Park
Wainwright Road
Warndon
Worcester WR4 9FA
Tel: 0121 609 0099
www.unifix.co.uk
Industrial clothing, tools and tool belts.

**Prinz Publications (UK) Ltd**
2A Hayle Industrial Park
Hayle
Cornwall TR27 5JR
Tel: 01736 751910
www.prinz.co.uk
Lindner finds display boxes.

**Eyemagnify Ltd**
PO Box 8107
Grantham
Lincolnshire NG31 9YE
www.eyemagnify.com
Magnifying glasses.

**Maplin Electronics Ltd**
PO Box 534
Manvers
Rotherham S63 5DH
Many branches throughout the United
Kingdom.
www.maplin.co.uk

# GOVERNING BODIES

## National Council for Metal Detecting (NCMD)
General Secretary
51 Hilltop Gardens
Denaby
Doncaster
DN12 4SA
E-mail: trevor.austin@ncmd.co.uk
www.ncmd.co.uk
Third party insurance is included with member-
ship. Contracts and agreements for landowners.

**Federation of Independent Detectorists (FID)**
Colin Hanson
'Detector Lodge'
44 Heol Dulais
Birchgrove
Swansea
West Glamorgan SA7 9LT
E-mail: fid.pro@detectorists.net
www.detectorists.net
Third party insurance is included with member-
ship. Contracts and agreements for landowners.

# SOCIETIES

## The Wyvern Historical and Detector Society
Please contact the author c/o the publisher for
more information.

# GOVERNMENT AND NATIONAL CONTACTS

## British Museum
Great Russell Street
London WC1B 3DG
Tel: 020 7323 8000/8299
E-mail: information@britishmuseum.org
www.britishmuseum.org

## Swindon Museum and Art Gallery
Bath Road
Swindon
Wiltshire SN1 4BA
Tel: 01793 466556
www.swindon.gov.uk

**Port Of London Authority**
Bakers Hall
7 Harp Lane
London EC3R 6LB
Tel: 020 7743 7900
www.portoflondon.co.uk

**Portable Antiquities Scheme**
Department of Portable Antiquities and
Treasure
British Museum
Great Russell Street
London WC1B 3DG
Tel: 020 7323 8611/8618
E-mail: info@finds.org.uk
www.finds.org.uk

# USEFUL DETECTING WEBSITES

Spanish coastal web cams.
wwwwebcam.comunitatvalenciana.com/web-cam-valenciaterraimar-cullera-24

Advice for Walkers and Country Code
www.maidstoneramblers.org.uk/Leaders'%20
Leaflet.htm

Metal Detectors Forum
wwwforumukdetectornet.co.uk/index.
php?id=117

Beach and In-water Safety
www.banthamslsc.co.uk/beach_safety_at_bantham.htm

RNLI Coastal Safety
www.rnli.org.uk/what_we_do/sea_and_beach_
safety/beachsafety/beach_safety
Global Weather Service
*www.weather.com/?from=globalnav*

Scrap Gold and Precious Metal Prices
www.cooksongold.com/metalprices/

Beach Metal Detecting
wwwfreespace.virgin.net/bob.bailey/Beach1/
beach5/bch5.html

SWAT Military Webbing
www.thearmystore.co.uk/acatalog/Viper_
Security_Belt_System.html

BBC Weather
www.bbc.co.uk/weather

Natural Lifestyle/Fitness Coaching
www.ukwellness.co.uk

# METAL DETECTING IN FRANCE

## *Periodicals*

*Le Fouilleur*
Monthly, 6.50 Euros
www.lefouilleur.com
Incorporates *L'or du Fouilleur*.

*Le Prospecteur*
Bi-monthly, 5.00 Euros
wwwprospecteur.1talk.net
Magazine of the Association Française des
Prospecteurs (AFP)

*Détection Passion*
Bi-monthly, 6.00 Euros
wwwpagesperso-orange.fr/detection.passion/
cadrsomm.htm

*Monnaies et Détection*
Bi-monthly, 5.50 Euros
www.loisirs-detections.com

## Associations

### Association Française des Prospecteurs (AFP)
wwwprospecteur.1talk.net

### Fédération Nationale des Utilisateurs de Détecteurs de Métaux ( FNUDEM )
www.prospection.net
The site also advertises their so-called School
of Detecting, which seeks to promote the metal
detecting cause to archaeologists and the general public alike. Some English translation is
available, albeit of dubious quality.

### Association Nationale pour la Détection de Loisir
www.detection-loisir.com

# INDEX

## GENERAL INDEX

air detecting 39
artefact 11, 32, 39, 42, 47, 49, 51, 83, 91, 122, 128, 145

battery 23, 27, 112, 113
beaches: in England 104; in France 105; in Spain 106
buddy system 56, 65, 115, 139

cleaning and presenting finds 112
clothing and ancillary equipment 67, 113
coils 23, 43, 49, 71, 113
community opportunities 12, 74
contacting landowners 81
contracts 82, 83

density 101, 102
disabled 21
displaying 131

equipment 67
equipment for use in water 111
Euros 8, 117
exercises 57
eyes only searching 15, 146

Federation of Independent Detectorists 76, 87, 155, 168
field walking 15, 146
first aid 61, 68, 70, 115

France 74, 93, 115, 116, 118
free finds service 12, 76, 78, 81, 105, 106

gloves 50, 51, 63, 114
gold 8, 10, 16, 39, 53, 84, 98, 104, 105, 117, 122, 125, 127, 128, 133–4, 138, 167
ground detecting 40

headphones 36, 67, 72, 115
historical society 76
hotspots 42, 43, 119
how to use your metal detector 36

i.d. card 76, 77
injections and medication 62
inland detecting 88
instructions 36, 38

jewellery 133
junk 24–5, 29, 39, 50, 51, 62–3, 96, 104, 141

lakes 13, 76, 106, 114, 116, 118
law 64, 84, 93

marker flag 29, 63, 66
Minelab 7, 10, 25, 29, 36, 112, 113, 166
money 104, 107, 108, 110, 122
Mudlarks 16, 152
munitions and weapons 64, 66

National Council For Metal Detecting 86, 169

permission 86–7, 89, 92–3, 136, 139, 141, 160
platinum 8, 133, 140–1, 143, 160
Portable Antiquities Scheme 86, 130
practice 24, 28, 39, 40, 49

recovery 47, 49, 51, 63, 67, 97, 112, 119, 154
research 12, 32, 74, 81, 88, 90–1, 103, 128
Roman 8, 90, 94, 122, 126–7, 139, 147–8

safely 13, 55, 66, 111, 114–15, 153, 156
sample contract 82–3
sampling 40, 45–6, 89
Saxon 8, 145, 149
Saxon Burials 141, 160
search patterns 41
signal 23, 47, 54, 57, 72
Silver 8, 10, 122, 125, 128–9
Spain 8, 54–5, 114, 119, 127
Swindon Museum 139–45

*The Scurcher* magazine 33, 166
tides 97–8, 100, 103, 108, 112, 154
tools 51, 67, 97
troubleshooting 54
Treasure Act 84, 190, 141
*Treasure Hunting* magazine 33, 166

underwater detecting 111

warm-up exercises 57
waves 102
White's 7, 10, 24, 30, 36, 166
Wyvern Historical And Detector Society 8, 139

# TECHNICAL INDEX

armrest 23

battery 23

care of detector 52
coil 23, 39–41, 43, 47, 49, 52, 71, 113
control box 23, 28, 52, 112–13

discrimination 24, 27–8

graphic display 28
ground balance 23, 27–8

motion detector 26, 28, 36, 41, 97, 112

numerical target display 23

PI detector 28–30, 96, 142
pinpoint 28, 47–9, 97, 142

sensitivity 25, 28, 54
single tone signal 24

TR detectors 27–8
troubleshooting 54

underwater detectors 31, 111, 133, 136

variable tone signal 24
visual target display 23, 25, 28

wet suit 114